God's Rainbow Book

Prayers and inspiration for the victims of Hurricane Katrina.

Introduction

⌒ ⌒ ⌒ ⌒ ⌒ ⌒

Hurricane Katrina's fury and devastation riveted the world's attention on the Gulf Coast for one harrowing week in late August, followed by the grisly aftermath of rescue and cleanup. But while many rushed to meet the physical needs of the survivors, Christian print-on-demand publisher Xulon Press has found a way to meet the spiritual needs of those whose homes and lives were ravaged by Katrina—in the form of this book, written by people all across America.

"As a Christian book publisher, we can't offer the victims food and water, but we can offer spiritual sustenance through the Word," Tom Freiling, president and CEO of Xulon Press, said. So we asked believers across America to help us write a book offering victims encouragement and inspiration. For every book we sell, we're donating two copies to the victims of the hurricane, and the company plans to donate all proceeds from the sale of the books to getting copies into the hands of victims.

After facing a disaster of biblical proportions, the survivors of Hurricane Katrina will need the kind of inspiration only God can provide. Without hope and faith, imagine how easy it would be to sink into despair. For some, starting a new life will mean starting from scratch; it won't be easy to get back on their feet. Xulon Press invites you to help place this hope-

inspiring book into the hands of a hurricane survivor by pur-
chasing a copy of this book, which reminds the hurricane victims of God's wonderful promises given in the account of
Noah's flood:

> And God said, "This is the sign of the covenant I am
> making between me and you and every living creature
> with you, a covenant for all generations to come: I have
> set my rainbow in the clouds, and it will be the sign of
> the covenant between me and the earth. Whenever I
> bring clouds over the earth and the rainbow appears in
> the clouds, I will remember my covenant between me
> and you and all living creatures of every kind. Never
> again will the waters become a flood to destroy all life.
> Whenever the rainbow appears in the clouds, I will see
> it and remember the everlasting covenant between God
> and all living creatures of every kind on the earth."

Genesis 9:12-16

Katrina, Katrina, God Cares for Your Victims

Powerful walls of the storm coming to the land
In her powerful winds she crossed over the sand
She came a storming, wreaking destruction to all
Oh God, oh God, hear our voices, our call

In our America came much sadness to all
Watching the news, time slowed to a crawl
What can we all do, our hearts crying with you
Praying each day, we are all suffering too

It is near over except all the people are scattered
Each man and woman is tired and tattered
Now we reach out our hands and our hearts to help
Come to our cities that we can share some wealth

Oh God, please come to each and every soul
Joy and healing, suffering won't take its toll
Let us all rise together with God in our hearts
And bring to each one some love and new starts

Praying now Father, oh Lord, bless our land
Becoming humble, bringing healing in our hand
Let each and every need be cared for by You
Knowing in the storms of our life, You are there too

Bless us as we care for our own sisters and brothers
Each and every child, bring to them their mothers
We love You, we are all Your children Lord
Loving one another let Your Holy Spirit pour

To the needs of the many, Your wonderful plan
One nation under God taking our stand
Loving one another, let You Lord rule in this story
Let all of us live together in the hope of Your glory

Let Us Pray

Father, thank You for being our God and hearing our prayers and the knowing that You will be with us and help in our time of need. The Bible states to first seek the kingdom of God and His righteousness and the things we need shall be added to us. We know the kingdom of God and His righteousness in us comes from the death of Jesus at Calvary. We know You see us through the blood of Jesus. The Bible states that we can do nothing without You but in You we have life and life more abundantly. It states Jesus came to destroy the works of the devil.

We know that like with Job much suffering comes and is allowed by God with the devil accusing us daily before Him. This was to prove that Job would not curse God. He would not deny God even though he lost all that he had. Even his friends thought he must be doing something wrong. Let us not turn away from but to You Lord God. Father, look past what we have all done and been, and grant us mercy. By Your hand Father we know that everything bad can be turned to good. I pray that we all can be led by You in this tragedy and bring forth good as all good things come from You.

Lord, pour Your Holy Spirit presence on these people and us in their hour of need. Let Your presence be strong, direct our steps and clear our path before us that Your glory will be seen. Let this event bring many to You, oh God, that they can receive the blessing of eternal life. Holy are You Lord and worthy to be praised. Father let us all live the new commandment Jesus gave to love one another, and as Jesus said when asked what is the greatest scripture in the Old Testament, let us love God with all our heart, soul, strength, and mind and our neighbor as ourselves. These victims of Katrina are our neighbors. The Bible says to humble ourselves before God and in due time we shall be exalted, and it says that all things turn to the good for those that love the Lord. Let us all submit to God and rededicate or for the first time give our hearts to the Lord. AMEN

DJ Shrewsbury
Tucson, AZ

Memo of Love

When it seems
No one can understand
Your sorrow and your pain—
When you see
All the devastation
Left by the hurricane—
Know that God
Loves YOU and will guide you
Throughout the coming years
And His love
Shines through neighbors worldwide
Who want to dry your tears!

God bless you!

Margaret R. Sikes
Apopka, FL

Thank you for letting us
Share in your pain
We do find God's face
In each of your names

As sisters and as brothers
I do have to believe
This bad thing that happened
Was sent to relieve

Your hurt and your struggles
To just have a life
Now we can see you
For much of your strife

Our hearts do we wrap you
Your arms we will give strength
Your courage inspires us
Your spirits are a gift

We welcome you into
Our cities and our homes
And hope while you're with us
You'll not feel alone

Do know that like God
We've carved you as well
Into the palms of
our hands and our hearts

You are our blessings
And so is your need
You allow us to do good things
And lead us to kneel

In prayer for thanksgiving
For the blessings we have
And now we can share these
With you in your despair

Do know we love you
Black, white, red, and green
Christian, Jew, and Muslim
For us we're the same

For God did He make us
In image and in likeness
And when we do see you
We see into His brightness

God of our fathers
Abraham's voice heard
Do bless us in this gift
Of people in their need

Amen

Ernest de l'Autin
Author, *Reach to the Wounded Healer* and *Of the Oaks*
www.ernestdelautin.com
Nederland, TX

God Is Good

One truth that comes shining through, when we consider the tragedies that occur, is that God is good. God has wonderful and comforting works towards people. Hurricane Katrina, which hit the southeast United States in August 2005, shows, for example, how God moves His people to respond to disasters. It is God who is in control. It is God who brings the strength to the needy in distress. It is God who provides a refuge from the storm.

> "For You [God] have been a strength to the poor, a strength to the needy in his distress, a refuge from the storm" (Isaiah 25:4a).

Christians have genuine God-given compassion for the victims and their families. God's people show the best qualities of being a believer in Christ by caring for and helping those in need. When God brings relief and strength to those in distress, it is another reason to be thankful to Him.

Oh, how good it would be for people to realize that it is God who is bringing them a refuge from the storm. The thankfulness should be ultimately directed to the Lord God instead of to the government and secular entities, which God may use to show His mercy.

God works through His people to minister and provide practical help to hurting victims. In the aftermath of Hurricane Katrina, many Christians and Christian organizations quickly responded to the call for help. Some of these Christian ministries included: Rescue Task Force, Mission Aviation Fellowship, Samaritan's Purse, World Vision, and many others, including Christian churches.

If you ask any of these Christians, "Why and how do you do this?" they will reply, "It is God who guides us, provides the means and deserves the credit!" When people are in need, God brings the relief and moves His people to demonstrate mercy and help. How wonderful is our God. How thankful we are for His sovereign works.

"Then they cry out to the LORD in their trouble, and He brings them out of their distresses. He calms the storm, so that its waves are still. Then they are glad because they are quiet; so He guides them to their desired haven. Oh, that men would give thanks to the LORD for His goodness, and for His wonderful works to the children of men!" (Psalm 107:29).

Wesley Mountain
Author of *Who Is in Control?, Amazing Ride* and four other books by Xulon Press
Rancho Mirage, CA

Strength Through Adversity

Through adversity I've learned so much,
About truth and virtue and right and wrong.
I don't claim to be a giant among men
But a little adversity will make you strong.

The Bible tells us that He won't place,
More upon us than we can stand.
Troubles and trials strengthen our faith,
When we place our cares in the Master's hand.

The way we handle troubles and trials,
Is a testimony to God's awesome power.
It's God's way of preparing us,
For the final trumpet at the final hour.

Jesus will help shoulder the load,
And help us become stronger and fitter.
With His help we can overcome,
And never become a bitter critter.

Ethan Moses
Madison, AL

Psalm 28:7 says, "The Lord is my strength and my shield; my heart trusted in him, and I am helped." Fifteen months ago our family experienced a tragedy that changed us forever. My middle son, Geoffrey, died after being run over by a car. That was our "storm." But be encouraged by the verse above, as we are living proof that GOD KEEPS HIS PROMISES. We've held fast to God's hand and He has sustained us and lifted us up and we praise him for his goodness, even though we don't always understand why things happen the way that they do. Friends, remember to pray daily for the Lord to be your strength. Trust in Him and you will be given power beyond anything available to you on earth...supernatural power to overcome, power to continue to press onward and upward. Read the 23rd Psalm every day, embrace it, believe it, and have faith that GOD IS WITH YOU ALWAYS.

Gay L. Simpkins
Nashville, TN

Father, I pray that this will be a wake-up call to everyone. With you there is hope, but without you there is none. You can make good out of any situation. I pray that many people will accept Jesus Christ as their Lord and Savior. Thank you for the emergency shelters. Help for people to be able to move back into their homes real soon. When everything is fixed, I pray that everyone will say "Thank you" because without you nothing is possible. In Jesus' name, amen.

This hurricane proves that your next breath is not guaranteed. Do you know where you will be spending eternity? It's a nice feeling to know that no matter what I'll go to heaven when I die. Works, religion, money or anything else won't save you. Ephesians 2:8-9 says, "God saved you by his special favor when you believed. And you can't take credit for this; it is a gift from God. Salvation is not a reward for the good things we have done, so none of us can boast about it." Just believing won't save you. Romans 10:9 says, "For if you confess with your mouth that Jesus is Lord and believe in your heart that God raised him from the dead, you will be saved."

If you said that prayer and meant it, congratulations! God wants a relationship with you. The way you will grow closer to God is by reading out of the Bible and praying to God. As you're tempted to do wrong remember these verses: James 4:7, "Resist the devil, and he will flee from you." Philippians 4:13, "For I can do everything with the help of Christ who gives me the strength I need."

God bless you.

Gretchen Gentry
Atlanta, GA

I rejoice in Jesus my Savior. He has come to bind up the bruises of His people, to set the captives free, to bring life more abundantly. He comes bringing restoration and healing to the House of Jacob, to deliver it out of all its troubles. He has come to rebuild David's fallen tent, to establish His tribe—the Tribe of Judah, to set it high upon His throne. Kings and queens of all nations shall marvel and be in awe at what the Lord has done. His Kingdom shall last forever.

Sylvia A. Thomas
Tallahassee, FL

Never!

It's okay to ask the question "WHY?"
It's even okay if you need to "CRY."
It's okay to fail sometimes, if you try.
But NEVER, ever let hope and belief die!

Michael Epps
Harvym, IL

Where Are You, God?

Where are You, God? Do You hear me crying? Do You see my tears? Do You know how much I've lost? Do You realize that my heart is breaking? Where are You, God?

My child, I am right here beside you. I hear you crying, and I see your tears. I know how much you've lost, and I realize that your heart is breaking. My heart is breaking for you. But know that I love you, and I will bring you through this terrible tragedy. I have created you with the skills to survive. You were born with courage, strength, and hope. These powerful attributes will help you to succeed in the months and years ahead. Trust Me. Believe Me when I say, "I know the plans I have for you, plans to prosper you and not to harm you, plans to give you hope and a future" (Jeremiah 29:11). "You are precious and honored in my sight, and…I love you" (Isaiah 43:4).

Ginnie Mesibov
Author, *Outer Strength, Inner Strength*
www.outerstrengthinnerstrength.com
Philadelphia, PA

God says to you, "Go to the depths of your souls to see the Lord, and all the goodness you will have to share. This is the Word of God. You must believe in yourself and you must believe in the power of the Lord God. For all that believe in this power supreme will share in the light of the Lord Jesus Christ. Do not be ashamed of your beliefs, or the faith you have in what you believe to be true. I am here for you. Hold the Bible and pray for solace, and I am here. The servants of the Lord will behold all the torment you are having, and you will not be alone. In all the Word, it is complete. See it, say it, and it shall be done. Do this is my name. Amen."

Debra DiMartino Wright and Fran Perricone DiMartino
Canton, GA

He Cares

"When I look at the sky, which You have made, at the moon and the stars, which You set in their places—what is man, that You think of him; mere man, that You care for him?" (Psalm 8:3-4 TEV).

Although houses and things are gone, like Noah of old
Yet you still have the most important thing—your soul.
Belongings may've been shifted,
And you're moving places, yet one thing remains for sure—
the Rock of all ages

When wind and storm come, fret not
You've the Rock to cling on taut
He says to you, "Count it all joy when you encounter strife
Above all, you still have Me, and you've still the gift of life!"

Didn't He promise He'll give the resources
To rebuild and perhaps replace your "losses?"
Didn't He say He WILL help accomplish your task?
Despite the circumstances, trust and He'll act fast!

Like the psalmist, look at the sky:
At the moon, sun and stars which lie
As constant and unmoved as they all have been,
Ever at Christ, who's the same now, yesterday and forever.

At the end of every day, you will savor
His steadfastness and everlasting favor
In your life and heart, give God praise
May He increase, and you He'll raise.

Give thanks, because He's shown mercy to you
God still cares; in fact, He still thinks of you.
Right up there, you WILL abide
In His pow'r and love, you'll hide.

By Kaiwen Chee and Ray Chee, author of
The Amazing Heart: A Revolutionary View That Could Save &
Lengthen Your Life!
Singapore

Undivided Waters

From the shores of the Mississippi to the lakes of New
Orleans, the waters are undivided
Undivided as the devil's foothold
But ne're shines a rainbow
Though the waters be divided
The Spirit of New Orleans remains

Quarantined though it may be the resolve will be the same
Lives and situations of despair
Nobody knows where it will all end
But God knows

God knows the lives that have been split up
God knows the lives that have been lost
But most of all God knows the end of the matter
The Spirit of New Orleans remains

By the wayside, by the wayside
The waters may recede but the fact remains
Lives were lost here and why were they lost here?
They were lost here for the sake of others

A whole future of others

Lee McCrorie
California, MD

New Life

Keep that old keeping
Keep that old regretting
Into the past always peeping
Things behind worth forgetting

Look forward to the light
See new life ahead
Begin to do that which is right
For that which is behind is dead

Freedom is a price
Lost in slavery past
Everything is yours that's nice
Rules of living in stone are cast

Others count our choice
We now are free
Hearken as you hear love's voice
Roots us firm as the old oak tree

Lose that old keeping
Lose that old regretting
Into the soul you will find seeping
Wings to fly when you're forgetting

Rev. J. A. [Jim] Watson B.Th.
Tofield, Alberta, Canada

A Prayer of Hope

There are times in life
when we aren't sure why.
Is there a God, a Creator who is looking nigh?

Why must turmoil, tragedy, and trial occur?
Wish life could be happy and always pleasing and filled with
    myrrh!

But it is in the times of testing and trial with heartache of life
That God helps us transition
and propels us to our destined plight.

Triumphant are we, when we see God's hope in the midst of
    a storm.
Overcomers are we—when we unite as one.
It's His leading and guidance that brings the calm.

For there are questions without answers, and answers that are
    merciless—
with seemingly no means to cope.
Which leads us to know—there is but One who is sovereign!
In Him is our hope.

Sonia Andriette Milner Adams
Lithia Springs, GA

Rain Rain Go Away

Rain rain go away,
Come back another day.

Rain rain go away,
Why did you come to stay?

Rain rain go away,
My life now I contemplate.

Rain rain I understand,
God's hand will take command.

Reign reign every day,
Thy kingdom, don't delay.

Reign reign every day,
Thy kingdom, don't delay.

Kim Antoinette Hatton
Houston, TX

Oh, Hurricane Katrina

You caught us unaware and inflicted pain unprecedented
in modern-day America. You have created pain and suffering
almost comparable to the great floods of history on a biblical
scale. Katrina, we are going to rebuild our lives, homes and
national unity. Divine love will return to our land. We ask the
Lord to provide healing to our land and help our emotional
turmoil.

For those taken home prematurely by Katrina, they are not
gone forever. Like a ship, we watch them disappear from the
sea shore. Someone says, "There, she's gone." But has she
gone? No, just at the moment when someone says, "She's
gone," another voice on a distant shore shouts, "She's here!"
Death is similar. Earth's loss is eternity's gain. Each of us has an
endless existence, first in this world, and then in the next.

Our thoughts and prayers go to the families of those who
have changed their earthly location for the new world. Our
prayers are with those suffering in the aftermath of the hurricane. May you be comforted in your grief by these words of
encouragement. May you receive help from the one who can
provide permanent and lasting help to mankind.

New Orleans: You are not alone, all the nations are with
you and the divine love enfolds you. May you know His love
that casts out all fear. Love is good, and nothing truly good
can perish. Let the power of love drive you back to God, who
is love.

"I have loved you with an everlasting love; I have drawn you with loving-kindness. I will build you up again and you will be rebuilt, O Virgin Israel" (Jeremiah 31:3-4).

The purpose of the above quote from the Bible is to be a source of encouragement that hope will never fail as we release our real loss, fear and anxiety to the Lord. Where there is hope, there is life. He will build His nation again.

Akeem Shomade
Author of *The Fear Factor*
Angel, London, UK

Now when he was in affliction, he implored the LORD his God, and humbled himself greatly before the God of his fathers, and prayed to Him; and He received his entreaty, heard his supplication, and brought him back to Jerusalem into his kingdom. Then Manasseh knew that the LORD was God (2 Chronicles 33:12-13).

And the LORD restored Job's losses when he prayed for his friends. Indeed the LORD gave Job twice as much as he had before (Job 42:10).

For God did not send His Son into the world to condemn the world, but that the world through Him might be saved (John 3:17).

For I know that my Redeemer lives, and He shall stand at last on the earth; and after my skin is destroyed, this I know, that in my flesh I shall see God (Job 19:25-26).

The LORD bless you and keep you; the LORD make His face shine upon you, and be gracious to you; the LORD lift up His countenance upon you, and give you peace (Numbers 6:24-26).

At the Feet of Jesus (A Poem)

At the feet of Jesus, there is exaltation
At the feet of Jesus, there is no lamentation
At the feet of Jesus, flow streams of restoration
At the Feet of Jesus, receive healing and salvation

At the feet of Jesus, there is unspeakable solace
At the feet of Jesus, there is no hopelessness
At the feet of Jesus, find a perfect friend
At the feet of Jesus, find eternal protection

At the feet of Jesus, there is no fear or terror
At the feet of Jesus, there is solution for every error
At the feet of Jesus, find love without measure
At the feet of Jesus, find eternal treasures

At the feet of Jesus, there is a new covenant
At the feet of Jesus, there is grace before judgment
At the feet of Jesus, come with a heart of repentance
At the feet of Jesus, find new life and prudence

Daisy Augustine
Chatsworth (Los Angles), CA

Soothe Your Soul

Blessings may seem few right now. You've been uprooted, traumatized, hungry and tormented. Your worries must be overwhelming. Thanks to CNN, all of us feel personally involved. We watched the tragedy unfold and we felt and still feel your pain, fear and suffering. Blessings are in lives saved. Blessings are in the many helping hands and nurturing hearts surrounding you now. Open up to them and let them help you.

Family, friends and possessions have been lost. Shock, grief and depression may consume you right now. But as you slowly heal, you will find all of your precious memories stored safely and securely in your heart. Precious memories are love. God is Love. Your memories are safe and so are you.

This is a time to renew your faith. Be brave as you make new choices in this new beginning. You are not alone. You are one of many proud Americans who have lost everything and started over. In God we trust, and when we do we succeed. Ask God for direction, and when you truly believe He will show you the way.

Let your tormented soul be soothed by knowing so many of us care about you and are praying for your recovery. We as Americans have so much that we sometimes take our lives for granted. But deep down, we are proud of our heritage, proud of our accomplishments and proud of our freedom. We are truly all for one and right now You are the One.

Patricia Kramer
Grundy, VA

꙳

Great God, You have promised never to leave or forsake us. We plead that You will remember your children who are suffering so much because of Katrina. Your ways are beyond our comprehension. Yet, we know You care. Bring healing and supply with healing, mentally, emotionally, physically, materially, yes and spiritually. Take away fear and restore hope. And may some see Your face and discover Your will for their lives even through this terrible tragedy. I ask this in Your most holy name, amen.

Ralph R. Gardner
Mt. Juliet, TN

Only God Our Creator

No words describe our heart's gaping hole, that dark emptiness that fills Americans' mind, body, and soul. The tears, the grief, the anger, the fear, the questions, the emptiness we'll all recall for years. No words describe the horrifying sights that burn in our minds through the days and the nights. Families, colleagues, acquaintances, and friends whose lives were so tragically affected or came to an end. ONLY GOD OUR CREATOR has the strength to empower us to stand, to bring forth victory over the pain in and through our land. ONLY GOD OUR CREATOR, as we humble ourselves and pray, can fill our aching hearts with hope to live each day. ONLY GOD OUR CREATOR can empower and heal the tragic event on mankind that seems so unreal. No words describe the heartfelt thanks to all men and women whose work is service, regardless of rank. The courage, heroism, and valor that heralds their call is a lesson in sacrifice and love to each and to all.

No words describe the value and gift of life more precious than anything that money can buy. Now is the time to speak loud and clear, words of love, to all in your world, both far and near. ONLY GOD OUR CREATOR has the strength to empower us to stand to bring forth victory over the pain in and through our land. ONLY GOD OUR CREATOR, as we humble ourselves and pray, can fill our aching hearts with hope to live each day. ONLY GOD OUR CREATOR can empower and heal the tragic event on mankind that seems so unreal.

No words describe the urgency of the task that faces each of us as we are called to ask; How can I be of service and help? My love, care, and concern are deeply heartfelt! No words describe the darkness of that day, when lives were devastated in every way!

Heaven's love and mine wraps around you, each and every one. After all, we're brothers and sister made one through Christ, God's Son!

Carolyn Lynn Schwartz
Goldthwaite, TX

⌒ⸯⸯ ⸯ⌒

"Therefore do not worry, saying, 'What shall we eat?' or 'What shall we drink?' or 'What shall we wear?' For your heavenly Father knows that you need all these things. But seek first the kingdom of God and His righteousness, and all these things shall be added to you" (Matthew 6:31-33).

In trying times we are tempted to worry about our present situation. However, Jesus tells us not to worry about these matters. The word *worry* comes from the word *merizo* which means to divide into parts. When we worry we divide the whole picture of our life and put much more focus on our troubles of today and our immediate future. Thankfully, God has a different and much brighter perspective, which many times we cannot see through our pain and sorrow. God is the master artist of our lives. The reason He can see the whole picture is because He is the one who paints it. God creates beautiful landscapes after ravaging fires. He sends rainbows of promise after torrential storms. Because God seeks to unite, rather than divide, He sends people to support us and lift us up as part of His promise. Look around and see the people who have been sent by God to fulfill this promise. When we are tempted to worry, we need only to take these words of Christ to heart. As we unite, instead of divide, we open the doors for God's perfect love to add all things to us.

Brad J. Williams
Bay City, MI

When the twin towers in New York fell, Australians felt and shared your pain and anguish. Now many of you have lost everything in the devastating wake of hurricane Katrina. How can we ever fully understand and appreciate your loss? How do we respond to such a tragedy?

We pray for you who are suffering, as you struggle for life's necessities. We pray that your immediate needs will be met. We pray that your loved ones are all safe. We pray that God's people all over the United States and the world will join with you to bring healing and hope.

May you find the peace of God through these dreadful circumstances.

God is our refuge and our strength
A very present help in trouble
Therefore we will not fear
Though the earth be removed
And though the mountains be carried into the midst of
the sea

Though its waters roar and be troubled
Though the mountains shake with its swelling. Selah.
Psalm 46:1-3

Dennis Urbans
Melbourne, Victoria, Australia

In the Storm

Are You there, Lord? It is me.
Do You see the things I see?
Can You hear me?
Do You even know my name?
Can You see me?
Will You ever reach my pain?
Are You there?

From somewhere in the darkness,
As I cry myself to sleep,
I hear a Voice that softly calls my name.
A Voice that touches me so deep,
A Voice that knows my pain.
You are here.
You have not abandoned me.
You are near.
I know that I am free.

Tho' all around me there is chaos,
Destitution, and unrest,
I refuse to give up hope,
For I know that I am blessed.
You are still the King of Kings,
You remain upon Your throne,
You are my Shepherd, You are here, and I am not alone.

Londa Harpster and two of her children, Josiah (9) and
Danielle (12)
Pasco, WA

In the Bible, Psalm 46:1 states that "God is our refuge and strength, a very present help in trouble." Psalm 107:6 says, "Then they cried unto the LORD in their trouble, and he delivered them out of their distresses." Psalm 121:1-2 says, "I will lift up mine eyes unto the hills, from whence cometh my help. My help cometh from the LORD, which made heaven and earth."

At one time I experienced the loss of my livelihood and my home and had no financial resources or a place to live. The all and the everything that I can tell you is that God is an awesome God; He provided me with a job that I didn't look for; He provided a place for me to live, and the means for me to move into it. He may not come when you want Him, but He is always on time. All that I have said is a personal testimony. Just trust Him. Rest in His arms. Hold on to His unchanging hand for dear life.

The fact that you are able to read this book of encouragement is a sign that He loves you.

My prayer is that God will bless you above anything that you can imagine during these trying times, and when it is done that you will give Him the praise, the honor, and the glory.

Pat Harris
Hagerstown, MD

After the storm, the sun will show;
After the rain, the flowers grow.
Just as we know these things are true,
So also is the Lord's love for you.

Gain strength from knowing His eyes are upon you,
Lovingly watching all that you do;
You will rebuild and He will restore all that was lost,
Know that complete restoration is yours to have.
It is yours, for Christ has paid the cost.

Venetia Carpenter
Watauga, TX

How to Really Conquer Your Fears

It is important to overcome our fears, but how we overcome them is more important that simply overcoming them. The Bible assures us that God is faithful. It is God who strengthens you in the tasks and trials you face. You do not face your situations in life by yourself.

When I was in the Army, I had a particularly scary time during rappel training. Fear of heights was not the problem. My problem was being afraid of the equipment I was using. Although my mind agreed with what I had been taught, mainly that the rope and O-ring would more than hold my weight safely, I could not comprehend how a rope that was less than an inch thick would hold both me and almost 50 pounds of equipment without breaking.

I am sure the instructors got a good chuckle watching me on the rappelling tower. I would step out on the edge of the wall of the tower muttering under my breath, almost in desperation, "I can do all things in him who strengthens me" (Philippians 4:13, RSV).

Look at the example of David in 1 Samuel 17. David, a young shepherd boy, just happened to be delivering care packages to his brothers, who were on the front lines of battle in the war between the Hebrew nation and the Philistines. While there, David heard the boasts of the Philistine champion, Goliath. David quickly summed up the situation, and asked, "Who is this uncircumcised Philistine, that he should defy the armies of the living God?" Instead of giving in to fear, David looked to God and was strengthened by Him. While all the soldiers around him were quaking with fear, it was David, a non-soldier, who through his faith in the living God was bold and accepted Goliath's challenge.

Personally, I think David was afraid. David was only a human being. He had plenty of time to think about his situation. David totally trusted in God, and he refused to take counsel of his (and others') fears.

Listen to what David said to Goliath:

> "Thou comest to me with a sword, and with a spear, and with a shield: but I come to thee in the name of the LORD of hosts, the God of the armies of Israel, whom thou hast defied. This day will the LORD deliver thee into mine hand; and I will smite thee, and all this assembly shall know that the LORD saveth not with sword and spear: for the battle is the LORD's, and he will give you into our hands" (1 Samuel 17:45-47, KJV).

As taught in the *Field Manual on Military Leadership in the United States Army*, courage is not the absence of fear, but the ability to perform your mission in spite of your fear. David was afraid, but he overcame his fear to complete his mission. His mission wasn't simply to kill Goliath. His mission was to bring glory and honor to God. There is an old poem that says:

> If you think you are beaten, you are;
> If you think you dare not, you don't;
> If you'd like to win but think you can't,
> It's certain that you won't.
>
> If you think you'll lose, you've lost,
> For out of the world we find
> Success begins in a fellow's will;
> It's all in the state of mind.
>
> Life's battles don't always go
> To the strongest and fastest man;
> But sooner or later the man who wins
> Is the man who thinks he can.

Our problems in life sometime seem like giants in comparison to ourselves. Like David, you can overcome your fears by trusting in Jesus Christ, who strengthens you. Through Christ you can face trials, face adversity, and face your problems. You can defeat the giants who cause fear by having faith and trust in Jesus. You cannot do it on your strength alone. You must trust that God will support you, as the song says, "...through many dangers, toils and snares." As you step off onto the edge of the wall of life, He is more than strong enough to support you, no matter what happens. All you have to do is trust and believe.

Dr. Jon F. Dewey
Lawton, OK

That's Your M.O.!
John 2:1-11

One morning, God spoke to me by His Spirit and said that all of His children have an M.O. Immediately, I thought about the law enforcement term *modus operandi*—the way a person operates, one's characteristics—but that wasn't it. I asked the Father what M.O. stood for, and He reminded me about Jesus at the wedding in Cana. He said that when the people ran out of wine, there was a need and that was their M.O. I asked again what M.O. stood for, and He said it stood for Miracle Opportunity. Whenever a need arises, no matter what it may be, that's your M.O.! Remember the woman with the issue of blood (Matt. 9:20-22)? Remember the blind man (Mark 8:22-25)? Remember Lazarus (John 11:43-44)? They all had a need when Jesus performed a miracle, and God is no respecter of persons (Rom. 2:11).

Not many years ago, I was told a spot was found on my mammogram. After performing the mammography several times, the spot was still there, so I had to have a biopsy. At that point I had a need. I needed the healing power of God to overtake my body. After the biopsy, the doctor called me a couple of days later at work to say that the spot found was, in fact, benign. During this time, you have suffered great loss and affliction, but be encouraged. That's your M.O.! The Father told me that He also has an M.O., only it stands for Motivation & Opportunity. He said that what motivates Him is our faith, and it presents an opportunity for Him to do a miracle. So don't look at that situation or circumstance as it is, but see it as your Miracle Opportunity and trust in the Lord with all your heart (Prov. 3:5-6). Your faith will be His motivation to do a miracle in your life!

Deidre L. Blair
Dolton, IL

Faith is a gift from God that grows stronger as we use it. Ask God to give you the faith to trust Him to help you through each day and to use you to encourage others in these difficult days. "Some trust in chariots and some in horses, but we trust in the name of the LORD our God" (Psalm 20:7, NIV).

Robert Michael Edward Richards
Lytham St. Annes
Lancashire, England

Strength Through Adversity

Through adversity I've learned so much,
About truth and virtue and right and wrong.
I don't claim to be a giant among men
But a little adversity will make you strong.

The Bible tells us that He won't place
More upon us than we can stand.
Troubles and trials strengthen our faith
When we place our cares in the Master's hand.

The way we handle troubles and trials
Is a testimony to God's awesome power.
It's God's way of preparing us
For the final trumpet at the final hour.

Jesus will help shoulder the load
And help us become stronger and fitter.
With His help we can overcome
And never become a bitter critter.

Ethan W. Moses
Madison, AL

At this time when we are lost for words, we can go to the well-spring of God's Word for what we need. God promises that He will "never" leave us. Whatever help we need, He is there to give it to us, just as he promised. He knows the depth of pain in each heart and is standing ready to comfort. Just look up and take hold of Him in faith. He will come in and do what only He can do.

Gwendolyn L. Simpkins
Nashville, TN

For all of Katrina's victims, we offer our prayers.
We offer hope, and we offer love, from a Savior on high.
As descendants of Adam, we are all connected.
And we all share the same earth, and the same sky.
We feel compassion, we understand your cries
But please remember unconditionally,
Jesus loves you, my brothers and sisters,
and so do I.

John Michael Domino
Ft. Myers, FL

There Is Hope!

> "Blessed is the man who trusts in the LORD, and whose hope is the LORD" (Jeremiah 17:7, NKJV).

There is always hope in a world surrounded by sin, destruction and death. When we do not see hope, hope is still there, waiting on us to respond. Psalm 42:5-6: "Why am I so sad? Why am I so upset? I should put my hope in God and keep praising him, my Savior and my God" (NCV). Where there is pain and despair, hope is comforting us, giving us the strength we need to face another tomorrow. When there seems to be no hope, hope is still evident waiting in the background ready. Hope is not in what is lost. Hope is not in what was devastated and destroyed. Hope is in those who are living, who are living today and resting assured in the hope of tomorrow. What is hope? Hope is the loving arms of a Savior. Psalm 147:11: "The LORD takes pleasure in those who fear Him, in those who hope in His mercy" (NKJV). Hope is the caring glance of a loving God. Hope is help sent from others, whose hearts were nudged by the Holy Spirit. Hope is surviving knowing God knows what I am going through and is helping me to cope with today. Hope is the prayers and encouragement of a world brought together by tragedy. Hope is Christ, whose sacrifice gives light for a better world, a better life and hope for a better tomorrow. Isaiah 8:17: "And I will wait on the LORD, who hides His face from the house of Jacob; and I will hope in Him" (NKJV).

Julie K. Shirkey
Jacksonville, IL

37

God has a way of painting rainbows unaware.
With the sky for a scaffold, there's no limit to His art.
He outlines the clouds with yellow-pink lines
after a storm, to let us know
He's watching over us to save us from harm.
He overpowers all earthly trials, with loving smiles
He empowers His children. We can overcome all
things through Christ's strength.

Kaci Lane
Tuscaloosa, AL

"The light shines through the darkness, and the darkness can never extinguish it" (John 1:5 NIV).

It's a long hard road to recovery, from Hurricane Katrina's wrath. But with the light from above emerges hope and unconditional love. So Lord, let your light shine through the sea of darkness and despair. Guide your people and give them strength to endure and keep them in your care.

John Michael Domino
Fort Myers, FL

Sometimes we cannot understand why certain things happen to us in life or why we are faced with tragic situations, but please be assured and encouraged in knowing that God loves and cares about you. He knows what you are going through and He is there for you. It may seem or feel as if He's not present and that He has deserted you, but He has not. You are on God's mind and, as He promised in His Word, He will not leave you or forsake you (Hebrews 13:5).

In Matthew 25:35-40 Jesus said, "...for I was hungry and you gave Me food; I was thirsty and you gave Me drink; I was a stranger and you took Me in; I was naked and you clothed Me; I was sick and you visited Me; I was in prison and you came to Me.' Then the righteous will answer Him, saying, 'Lord, when did we see You hungry and feed You, or thirsty and give You drink? When did we see You a stranger and take You in, or naked and clothe You? Or when did we see You sick, or in prison, and come to You?' And the King will answer and say to them, 'Assuredly, I say to you, inasmuch as you did it to one of the least of these, My brethren, you did it to Me.'"

As you go through this period of time in your life wherein many prayers are being petitioned on your behalf, and love and care for you is being exhibited throughout the world, please find comfort in knowing that these deeds are the workings and manifestation of the Lord's glorious presence.

Keep your trust and faith in Him...God bless,

Runae L. Gary
Birmingham, AL

⁓ ᑕₑ ₛ⊃⁓

The news is broadcast over the airwaves, the most dreaded storm of the century. I have so many thoughts racing through my mind, what about family, friends, home? Now my worst fears have become a reality. I have suffered more than I could have imagined. Does anyone really care? My dear fellowman and friend, the fact you can even ask the question is the most precious blessing one could have, one's life. Everything except lost relationships can be replaced. You would be amazed at your ability to strengthen those around you by looking for opportunity in opposition. If you will absorb yourself in the needs of others, it will help you deal with your own personal loss. You, my friend, would be much more believable than anyone from the outside because you have faced the same tragedies as those around you. Allow the Lord to turn your tragedy into triumph. He is with you! And yes, WE CARE....our prayers and thoughts go with each of you in this time of your need.

Gordon Gainey, pastor
Zion Life Ministries
Camden, SC

⌒ᴄ₂ ₂ᴖ⌒

God wants to be our refuge during any storm, be them fiscal or emotional. The Bible reveals valuable lessons of how God responds to us in the middle of a storm. He can provide us with a refuge as he did with Noah. God told Noah to construct an ark for him and his family since a flood was coming. Since Noah obeyed, they had a place of refuge when the flood arrived. God closed the refuge leaving only a window with a view to heaven. That way they couldn't see the devastation that happened.

The ark is a symbol of Christ. When we trust in his gift of eternal salvation and keep the eyes of our faith in him, he becomes our ark of security against any kind of storm that life can bring us. He gives us strength and peace to overcome any difficulties. That peace comes because we know that we are not alone and that because he loves us he advised us that many signs were to happen before his second coming, such as wars, natural disasters, and hunger.

Even when these things happen you can find comfort knowing that his coming is near and every believer is going to be transferred to live in a place where there is no more tears, pain, death or floods. This day is close. And while it happens lets look upon the Lord, so we can endure and overcome with a strong faith any kind of storm, knowing that our liberation from this fallen world is about to happen. God wants you to be part of the eternal life with him. That's why he came to die for you and me, so that we can in turn live eternally with him. If you believe and accept Jesus as your Savior, you can start to live with confidence that you will have a part with him when he returns. Meanwhile he will bring you lots of internal peace, joy, and strength even in the middle of any kind of storm (Genesis 7:7).

Nilda Vazquez
Mayaguez, Puerto Rico

⌒⌒⌒⌒⌒

As I look at the pictures of the destruction and devastation that Hurricane Katrina has wrought, I feel such deep sadness and helplessness. I grieve for the families that have lost so much; I can only imagine their agony and pain. Our prayers have been for you and your loved ones, and that God will comfort and sustain you. We hope you will draw strength and encouragement knowing so many all over the world are praying for you and are concerned for your well being.

One thing that you can know with certainty: God knows and cares. We have His promise in 1 Peter 5:7: "Casting all your care upon Him, for He cares for you." Let God's words in the Psalms comfort you. "The Lord is near to those who have a broken heart, and saves such as have a contrite spirit" (Psalm 34:18). "God is our refuge and strength, a very present help in trouble. Therefore we will not fear, even though the earth be removed, and though the mountains be carried into the midst of the sea; though its waters roar and be troubled, though the mountains shake with its swelling" (Psalm 46:1-3).

How encouraging and thrilling to know that there is a home that God has built for us that can never be taken away or destroyed. If we let Him direct our lives, if we follow His teachings faithfully, He has promised that "an entrance will be supplied to you abundantly into the everlasting kingdom of our Lord and Savior Jesus Christ" (2 Peter 1:11). "And God will wipe away every tear from their eyes; there shall be no more death, nor sorrow, nor crying. There shall be no more pain, for the former things have passed away" (Revelation 21:4).

God bless you,

Carrie Coker Marrs
Rancho Cordova, CA

From Across the Nation

From across the nation, I see your tears
and pray that God will lift your sorrow.
My heart is broken as I see your destruction
and pray for a brighter tomorrow.
When there is no tangible hope
I pray that you will seek,
The true Hope that surrounds you
for it's Jesus who blesses the meek (Matthew 5:5).
When all your strength is gone
and you feel that life is through,
God says "do not fear...or be dismayed...
I will strengthen and help you" (Isaiah 40:10).
Although your days are hard
and I cannot fathom your pain,
I pray for your hope and salvation—
that you'd give your life for Jesus to reign.
The road ahead is rocky,
and the unthinkable you have braved,
Now let our God carry you,

for "Everyone who calls on the name of the Lord
will be saved" (Romans 10:13).
From across the nation I send my love
because in Christ, we are one.
From across the nation, I pray for you
in the mighty power of the Son.

May our Lord God give you strength, perseverance, and hope
during this time of great need. May He carry you through the
darkest hours and lift you up with the promise of His everlasting love, found in the glory of His Son, Jesus Christ. May the
sweet hand of our Savior wipe your tears and keep you safe. In
His sovereign name I pray, amen.

Robin Lynn Johnson
Modesto, CA

God Is Still Here

I can feel the hand of Satan, as he tempts me to the core.
He has asked my heav'nly Father for the right to tempt me
more.
And I heard the Father grant it saying, "Do not take his life.
Though you tempt him, he'll not stagger. He will rise above
the strife."

God has kept me through the desert. Jesus holds me in the
storm.
In the bitter winds of winter I am sheltered and kept warm.
Satan's anger rages round me, but his threats one day will end,
Silenced by the my heav'nly Father who my troubled soul will
mend.

Though I'm bruised, I'm not defeated. I still walk God's sunlit way.
And the comfort of His presence holds me fast. I cannot stray.
I look up and see His glory and the darkness opens wide.
Rays from heaven bring this promise: Jesus Christ is at my side.

Lord I trust you in the darkness and I praise you in the light.
There is nothing I can't conquer when it's you who leads the fight.

Elizabeth (Betty) Shepherd
Bonne Terre, MO

We Trust God

Broken down, plucked up, moved from our land,
Afflicted with evil, but we shall stand.
Though we've been shaken to our very core,
You, Lord, will build us and plant us once more.
In You we trust, Lord, and in You alone.
That You will deliver us and bring us back home.
The storm clouds look black when we stand far away,
But Your beauty emerges when we begin to pray.
In You, Lord, we'll find rest that we've never known,
For Your grace is flowing to us from Your throne.
Our hearts will stay set, even in this dark hour,
To stand on Your promises and depend on Your power.
We'll stand firm and strong, and learn of Your ways.
For Your hand is on us in these dark days.
Please, Lord, move swiftly for there is much to be done.
We rend our hearts and unite them as one.
We stand hand in hand and give no room to strife,
Because written on Your palm is each name, each life.

Help us not worry, help us not fret,
For we know that in Jesus' name our needs will be met.
We'll dwell not on how little or how great we may be,
But only on the power that we have in Thee.
So lead on, Lord Jesus, we are hearing Your call.
We'll follow Your voice, and we'll give you our all.

Donna Somers
Severn, MD

❧ ❦ ❧

When King Jehoshaphat was informed that several enemy forces were at his borders ready to attack the Israelite nation, he was alarmed. The people had no weapons or militia since they had been in bondage for so much of their history. However, the Israelites left us a wonderful example of how to respond positively in an emergency situation. In their calamity, they called on God. "For we have no power to face this vast army that is attacking us. We do not know what to do, but our eyes are upon you" (2 Chronicles 20:12). Because the Israelites obediently prayed and depended upon God, He assured them, "Do not be afraid or discouraged because of this vast army. For the battle is not yours, but God's" (verse 15). God instructed His people to march against the foe; they would not have to fight the battle because God promised to deliver them. As the Israelites marched toward the battlegrounds they prayed and praised, worshipping the Lord in the splendor of His holiness. True to His Word, God arranged for the two warring enemy forces to ambush each other. The Lord had given His people the victory and they rejoiced and praised Him.

There are many enemy forces in our lives today and most of us are ill-equipped to fight our own battles. Your current enemy is Hurricane Katrina, producing homelessness, poverty, and loss. Just as God promised His presence and His power centuries ago to a frightened, helpless people, He is still in the business of performing miracles in lives today. God will fight your battles; He only requests that you place your full faith and trust in Him. God's powers have not been diluted through the ages. He is still as strong as He ever was. Leave your frustration, fear, and future to the God of the universe who plans your life perfectly and in His precise timing.

God wants to fight your wars. Talk to God, expressing that you want Him to combat the widespread conflicts of devastation, deprivation, and despair. Then give Him your personal struggles of doubt, fear, weakness and worry. In His Word, God has promised repeatedly to meet all of your needs. God has more than enough love and strength to supply everyone.

Contrast this world's insecurity and volatile nature with God's unsurpassed love and peace beyond our understanding. Keep your eyes upon God. Allow Him to fight your battles and He will enable you to access the abundant life He promises!

Patricia Carver Knight
Belgrade Lakes, ME

The Very Same Flood

Out of devastation we rise to elevation for it is the very same flood that carries us to peaks of victory and summits of hope! That which furiously swept in to take away all is the very same flood that gave us a new beginning. Now! Look and see! The very same flood that stole is the catalyst for economic release. Families and friends broken apart by angry deluge acquire a deeper appreciation, value and respect because of the very same flood! So, hear and know that the very same flood that is your bane and fear shall become your greatest testimony! The very same flood!

Anya M. Hall
Orlando, FL

⌐⌐⌐

Seek the Lord in these trying times and know that His word is true. Psalm 9:9: "The Lord also will be a refuge for the oppressed, a refuge in times of trouble." In this world we see death as the end when in fact it is the beginning of life with our Father God in heaven—a place of love, peace and joy. No more pain, suffering or sickness. All are alive in Him. God is not the God of the dead, but of the living (Matt. 22:32). We are confident and willing to be absent from the body, and present with the Lord (2 Cor. 5:8). Trust in the Lord. God's blessing be with you.

Eric L. Paschal
Decatur, GA

I Am at Work in Your Life

"Hear me when I call, O God of my righteousness: thou hast enlarged me when I was in distress; have mercy upon me, and hear my prayer."

The good news is that He who created you and loves you has already heard your pleadings and is on the way to send His mercies to you. Although you may not see His grace in your actual circumstances, He is already at work in your life through (word through in italics) your circumstances, to enlarge you and to make you stronger and better, not weaker and bitter.

You are where you are so you may learn to grow in love, compassion, godly character and patience. Trust with all your heart that God is leading your ways, regardless of your present circumstances. Repeat to yourself time and time again, "God is my helper and He is in control at this very moment, even in my present circumstance."

This crisis can make you bitter or better; the choice is yours. Instead of becoming a victim, choose to become a victor. Instead of becoming discouraged, choose to encourage someone else. Instead of losing your hope, choose to dream big dreams. Choose to dream of the possibilities of new and better things to come. Remember that every adversity hides the seed of the opportunity of a new and better beginning.

Instead of dwelling on your present situation, choose to dwell and believe that God loves you and has a plan for you. In Jeremiah 29:11-12 God is saying to you: "For I know the plans I have for you," declares the LORD, "plans to prosper you and not to harm you, plans to give you hope and a future." He promised it to you and He will deliver, if you believe Him and put your trust in Him.

Instead of choosing to be depressed, choose to invest in other people's lives, right there where you are. As you help others you will not only feel much better about yourself, but you will discover unconditional love through service. You will find out that your purpose in life, the reason to be here, is to magnify the love of God on earth through helping others.

He is already working in your soul and material prosperity; He is protecting you from harm (think about it, you are alive and your *basic* needs are being taken care of). He is already working in your hope, if you trust that He loves you and that He is in control of your circumstances. He is also waiting to give you a glorious future, if you acknowledge Him and allow Him to help you make the right attitude choices.

As this crisis arise and extend, don't faint and give up. Refuse thoughts of entitlement and victimization. This tragedy may pave the way for you to find out your purpose and legacy in life and to find God in your life. Believe God is at work in your life today, as He is.

Candido Segarra
Plantation, FL

When Crises Occur...

The mind wants to know WHY - Why me? The heart wants to know WHEN - When will the pain go away? The will wants to know WHAT - What are my choices? Which direction should I take? Justice wants to know WHO - Who do I blame? The human spirit wants to know WHERE - Where is God in all of this? God is Love (1 John 4.8) and Love answers...I am not the cause, but I am the ANSWER. (May you be comforted and strengthened by the people God uses to help you, comfort you, encourage you, and love you through this period of transition.)

Jacqueline J. Wright
Decatur, GA

Bloom Where You're Planted

Like floodwaters seep behind locked doors, God's Spirit knows no bounds. He bids you to a calling only you can fulfill, because of who you are and what you have been through.

It was a blustery spring morning the day my husband and I traveled through a decaying neighborhood. Neglected homes with peeling paint and cracked windows echoed despair. But something amazing caught my eye. Next to an abandoned house a towering camellia bush blazed with brilliant fuchsia blossoms. Breathtaking in any garden, fit to grace a mansion, its magnificence was intensified by the drabness of the setting. I marveled at the proud plant flourishing where it had been planted. The beauty I'd enjoyed for only moments remains vividly etched in my memory.

My natural tendency is to rationalize that conditions must be perfect before trying new things. However, my perspective changed one afternoon when a package arrived in the mail. It held a box of plants that I'd ordered from a catalogue. To my dismay the spindly twigs, dried seeds, and shriveled bulbs hardly resembled the lush blossoms pictured in the gardening catalogue.

The pictures were intended to spark a vision of what my garden might look like, with a lot of hard work and tenacity on my part. It would be up to me to prepare the soil, plant the ugly twigs, drop bulbs into holes, water the seedlings, fertilize struggling plants, and pull the obnoxious weeds. Hopefully my patience would be rewarded with something remotely resembling the pictures in the seed catalogue.

Realizing one's dreams requires a vision to cling to, an ideal to strive for, and a picture in the mind. Tragedy, storms, death, and disease often rob us of our envisioned future. With God's help we can replant our dreams with the twigs of our life experience, the bulbs of enlightenment, and the seeds of faith that complete our make-up.

The only difference between a success and a failure is that when a failure falls down he gives up. When a successful person falls down he gets back up and tries again. It's called determination. It's blooming where we are planted.

"This is what the Lord Almighty, the God of Israel, says to all those I carried into exile from Jerusalem to Babylon: 'Build houses and settle down; plant gardens and eat what they produce. Marry and have sons and daughters; find wives for your sons and give your daughters in marriage, so that they too may have sons and daughters. Increase in number there; do not decrease. Also, seek the peace and prosperity of the city to which I have carried you into exile. Pray to the Lord for it, because if it prospers, you too will prosper'" (Jeremiah 29:4-7).

Carol Genengels
Seabeck, WA

⌒⌒⌒

(A prophetic word was given to this author August 28, 2004, one year prior to Katrina)

"Come up higher...as surely as I am the Lord God of Israel, storms are coming...Oh hold Me up saith the Lord. Hold Me up in the high places saith the Lord. Do not be shaken; do not be afraid...integrity is your weapon. Praise and worship is your weapon.

Listen one that has gone through the storm, listen dear one that has gone through the battle. Thus saith the Lord: you did not go through it alone. I was with you. I am with you now, even now, don't look unto your own devices, and don't look unto your own methods.

Oh My wounded one, I am next to you in this hour, I, even I look into the hearts of all men, and I see clearly. I do see your wounds. I do see your condition saith the lord.

Listen to me saith the Lord. I am love. Do you need love in this hour saith the Lord? I am love. I am love - I am what you need. I will not forsake you.

This is not an accident, this thing that has happened to you. My child my dear child, reach out to me in spirit. I will teach you, reach out to me in spirit and I will embrace your spirit with my love, for it is My love that you need in this hour.

Repent from all strongholds, turn from any wicked way and I will cause your situation - yes, Yes, I will cause your situation to turn around for you on your behalf. For I am the Lord God of Israel and nothing My child, nothing My dear sweet child whom I love, nothing is too difficult for Me. Can't you trust Me? Won't you let Me love you? Reach out to Me and I will touch your heart in this very hour saith the Lord".

Clinton Clark
Rochester, NY
Parts reprinted with permission from *Betrayed by Gossip* by Clinton Clark
(Xulon Press)

Take Heart

How many times in the course of your life
Have you tried, but the chips were down?
How many dreams in the hope they'll come true
Have you dreamt, with no hope for a crown?

But must you at standstill,
Stop trying, stop dreaming,
Stop planning and striving,
Stop living, stop breathing?

Do you know of a tide that stops ebbing,
Stops flowing,
Or a breeze though so light,
That will ever stop blowing?

The tide and the breeze,
Of God's plan are a part,
How much more are you?
You've got to take heart.

Susan Justina Wallace
Freeport, Grand Bahama
Bahamas

We Will Remember!

No words can remove all the pain. No song can wash away
all the sorrow. No brief comfort can replace all the lifetime
we have lost.

We will remember!

When the horror of tragedy strikes, we are beaten down. Our
despair is unlike anything we've ever known. We struggle to
deal with the here and now.

We will remember!

But in time…we will also remember the smiles of those we
loved and who loved us. We will remember the joys we
shared, the homes we built, the friends and neighbors we
laughed with.

We will remember our fathers and mothers, our brothers and
sisters, aunts, uncles, cousins, relatives of blood, of marriage,
of heart. We will cling to our memories and cherish them
forever. And we will ignore those who tell us to leave our past
behind and get on with life. No!

We will not! We will carry our thoughts, our dreams, and our hopes as we build our new tomorrow. We will not forget.

We will remember!

And in our grief...though slowly it may come...we will remember Him, too. We will remember His promise that regardless of the difficulties of life in this world...He is with us! Regardless of the pain we suffer...He is with us! Regardless of the sorrow and the countless, countless tears...He is with us!

We will remember!

We have heard Him in the voices that called us to safety. We have seen Him in the eyes that looked to our needs. We have felt Him in the arms that reached out to hold us. We have known Him in the hearts, souls, minds, and strength that encouraged us and saved us in the fury of the storm.

We will remember!

For one day we will be called on to help those who will be as we are now. It will be our time to come in their hour of need. It will be our time for others to hear, see, feel and know His love that lives inside of us and grows with each passing moment, as we carry them out of the darkness and into the light of a bright new day. We will stand together and we will stand strong...because God will be with us still.

We will remember!

"And surely I am with you always, to the very end of the age" (Matthew 28:20).

Take care and be God's.

Charles B. Graham
Executive Director
Ciloa...Encouraging one another as long as it is called Today!
Lawrenceville, GA

⌢ℭ ℈⌢

If you must cry, cry knowing that God will wipe the tears away and let those tears turn to praise knowing that "you are still here."

Feel like shouting? Yell to the rooftop. Let your shouts turn to praise knowing that "you are still here."

Soon and very soon you will be able to look back and say, "My soul looks back and wonders how I got over." And when you look back and see those one set of footprints in the sand, know that it was God who was carrying you then, and it is God who is carrying you now.

Isabel Emerson
Richmond, CA

⌢ℭ ℈⌢

To all the dear people who have suffered so greatly in this tragedy. To all who have lost loved ones in this calamity, Jesus has not turned his face away from you. Through every forest fire, new growth appears in the field. You can still see scars of the fire, but that only shows you something happened at some point. Scars don't prevent new growth. Psalm 3:3-4 says, "But Thou O Lord, art a shield for me: my glory, and the lifter up of mine head. I cried unto the Lord with my voice, and he heard me out of his holy hill. Selah."

Selah means "pause and think deeply on this." Our God

doesn't sleep. Keep your faith in the Ancient of Days. It is probably difficult to praise the Lord in this calamity you face, but praise the Lord anyway. He will respond to you.

Keith Miller
Vienna, OH

Help me, Jesus, through this day
In my work and in my play
I will do my very best
God will handle all the rest

Pain and tears will come along
Their lessons will make us strong
Look for good in all you see
Holding on to Jesus is the key

He will take me by the hand
Together we can make a stand
My future is mine to choose
With my Friend, Jesus, I can't lose!

Yea, God!

Nick Della Valle
Orange, CA

We submit to you God's promise to Israel found in Isaiah 54: 5-14. May you find comfort in this prophetic word to you. For thy maker is thine husband; the Lord of hosts is his name; and thy Redeemer is the holy one of Israel; The God of the whole earth shall he be called. For the Lord hath called thee as woman forsaken and grieved in spirit, and a wife of youth, when thou wast refused, saith thy God. For a small moment have I forsaken thee: but with great mercies will I gather thee. In a little wrath I hid my face from thee for a moment; but with everlasting kindness will I have mercy on thee, saith the Lord thy Redeemer. For this is as the waters of Noah unto me: for as I have sworn that the waters of Noah would no more go over the earth, so I have sworn that I would not be wroth with thee, nor rebuke thee. For the mountains shall depart, and the hills be removed; but my kindness shall not depart from thee, neither shall the covenant of my peace be removed, saith the Lord that has mercy on thee.

O thou afflicted, tossed with tempest and not comforted, behold, I will lay thy stones with fair colors, and lay thy foundations with sapphires. And I will make thy windows of agates, and thy gates of carbuncles, and all thy borders of pleasant stones. And all thy children shall be taught of the Lord; and great shall be the peace of thy children. In righteousness shalt thou be established, thou shalt be far from oppression; for thou shalt not fear: and from terror; for it shall not come near thee.

Blessed be the name of the Lord and may you find rest and strength for your weary soul in Him, His word, and His power.

Blessings,
Hope D. Blackwell & the Back to the Garden Ministries
Family
Norfolk, VA

Where was God when all this happened? God's original plan for you was that you live in paradise. We don't live there anymore and tragedies, such as Hurricane Katrina, happen. Just as Jesus wept with Mary and Martha at the death of their brother Lazarus, He now weeps with you in your pain and confusion. And just as He comforted them with His presence, He longs to comfort you and heal you, right in the middle of you confusing circumstances. He understands your hurt, sorrow and anger; even when you're angry at God himself and blame Him for it all.

All that He will carry for you, when you open it up and pour it all out to Him. He understands, better than any person ever can, the waves of pain and bewilderment that crash upon you time after time. He never grows tired or impatient of hearing you telling Him everything again and again until His comfort begins to trickle down into your heart and you begin to heal.

Arline Westmeier
Grantsville, MD

⌒ᔕᣇ ᔞᔑ⌒

The rainbow of the New Testament is the cross of Christ. In contrast to the first rainbow, the cross signifies deliverance from the flood of sin and the storm of evil. The cross points to the grace of God made available when Jesus paid our sin debt by dying for us. "For the grace of God that brings salvation has appeared to all men" (Titus 2:11 NIV).

Whatever your situation you may rely on God's grace now. If you have depended on God's grace by receiving Jesus as your Savior and Lord, you may claim the promise of 2 Corinthians 12:9 (NKJV): "My grace is sufficient for you, for My strength is made perfect in weakness."

Take comfort also in the promise: "And the God of all grace, who called you to his eternal glory in Christ, after you have suffered a little while, will himself restore you and make you strong, firm and steadfast" (1 Peter 5:10 NIV).

Carroll E. Hamilton
Locust Grove, VA

⌒ⱱ⸗ ⸚⸏ ⌒

Dear friends in the Gulf Coast,

As I write this letter to you I am struck by the fact that I may never know or fully comprehend the suffering that you are going through. This is why I can not conceive of saying the all-too-cliché words "I understand." The fact is, I do not understand. Nor may I ever. To suddenly have your entire life ripped out from underneath your feet is something that can only be understood by those who have gone through it. I can only say that I care and that I am praying for you.

Although I may never understand, I can tell you one thing for sure. God understands. The great truth of Christianity is that the God of the Bible is the God who can relate to human suffering and frailty. How is this possible for God, who lives in heaven , to relate to the suffering of man?

The answer is that God has walked in our shoes. In the person of Jesus Christ, God wrapped Himself in human flesh and came to live with us for a while. Not only did He come to show us His character. He came to feel our pain. Perhaps you have seen the recent movie the Passion of the Christ. Suffice it to say that in the physical torture of the crucifixion along with the spiritual and emotional pain of isolation and abandonment, God experienced the entire gamut of human suffering on that dreadful day. Not only can God say that He cares; He can also say that He understands.

I have good news for you my friends. Not only does God understand; He has also provided a way to save you from this present evil world of suffering and hardship. The Bible says that Jesus "gave Himself for our sins so that He might deliver us from this present evil age." The good news is that Jesus did not stay in the grave. On the third day, Jesus rose triumphantly from the grave and ushered in a new era of hope for all of humanity. Jesus said, "Because I live, you can live also." Because He lives, I know that one day when I leave my physical body, I will enter into a new life of everlasting joy and peace in a real place called heaven. This is not simply a fool's hope for the weak and simpleminded. Over 500 people saw Jesus alive and well after the crucifixion. Many of them are named in the New Testament.

As you are in your stages of grief and mourning, remember that this life is but a breath. It is here today and gone tomorrow. Eternity is forever. As the Apostle Paul says, "Our light affliction which is but for a moment, works in us a far more exceeding and eternal weight of glory." With an eternal perspective, even a life time of grief is changed to a passing moment.

Friend, have you given your heart to Christ? If you would like to have assurance of your eternal destiny, you can start by saying a simple prayer. "Jesus. Come into my heart. Forgive me of my sins. I accept you." The Bible says that "if you confess with your mouth that Jesus is Lord and believe in your heart that God has raised Him from the dead, you will be saved." It really is that simple. It is man that tends to complicate things by adding human merit to the equation.

I would like to close with the words of Jesus. I believe that He can reveal His heart to you far better than I. So here are His words. "Come unto me all you who are weary and heavy laden and I will give you rest. Take my yoke upon you and learn from me. For I am meek and lowly of heart. My yoke is easy and my burden is light." May you find the burdens of life lifted from your shoulders as you draw close to Jesus in your time of grief.

Aaron D. Taylor
Hillsboro, MO

⁀ᘓᚷ ᔆᓬᔓ⁀

I can only imagine what you are feeling, so during this time of great grief and devastation I encourage you to stay focused on the promises of God for your life. The Lord declares to us in Jeremiah 29:11-14, "For I know the thoughts I think towards you, saith the Lord, thoughts of peace, and not evil, to give you an expected end. Then ye shall call upon me, and ye shall go out and pray unto me, and I will hearken unto you. And ye shall seek me, and find me, when ye shall search for me with all your heart. And I will be found of you, saith the Lord: and I will turn away your captivity, and I will gather you from all nations, and from the places whither I have driven you, saith the Lord; and I will bring you again into the place whence I caused you to be carried away captive."

God loves you and we do too. My family is diligently praying for your family. In the midst of it all focus on the gift of life and the promises of God and don't give up on Him, he won't give up on you. I have been to hell and back and I found out that He is who He says He is. Take one day at a time, expecting a miracle each day knowing that God is and shall be Jehovah Jireh, your provider. I hope this poem I wrote for you will encourage your heart.

Always With You

Lo, I am with you always forever
I will leave you never
At night when you close your eyes I'll lay right beside you
Each day I'll awake you and from the danger I'll hide you
I'm all around you, yet deep inside you

I'll take your breath away, while I breathe on you each day
I am your lion of Judah, at the same time your gentle lamb I
    am, that, I am
So much more, I'm the one who'll pour
Into your empty cup, I'll fill you up I'll change your life,
I'll remove the strife I'll take your blame, I'll take your shame
You will not be the same, I'll shall change your name

I was disgraced here, I took your place dear, but I'll give you
love here, a warm embrace here I'll plead your case, your
heart I'll pace and because of me, you'll win this race

Lo I am with you always forever
I'll leave you never
At night when you close your eyes I'll lay right beside you
Each day I'll awake you and from the danger I'll hide you
I'm all around you, yet deep inside you.

Though you turned away, I love you still
When your hope seems gone, I'll make you feel I'll give you love,
I'll give you peace I'll give you mercy that never ceases
My grace protects you, my hand directs you
My love affects you, I won't neglect you

They said they would, they never did
I was always there, I never hid
I always called, I always spoke
I never played you, I never joked
I walk beside you, forever in you
I'll always love you, I'm always with you

Lo, I am with you always forever
I'll leave you never
At night when you close your eyes I'll lay right beside you
Each day I'll awake you and from the danger I'll hide you
I'm all around you, yet deep inside you

Now sit back and observe, as your life I change
As I heal your heart, and remove your pain
As I give you value and I give you a new name
I'll give you purpose and an end to your shame
And you'll walk again in new strength, power, and might
As I snatch you from hell and turn your midnight to daylight

Then I'll send you forth unto the nations
To speak purpose and life to my creations
Until their hearts embrace,
Until their hands raise,
Until their names change,
Until they sing praise
Until you proclaim that I am the same
Yesterday, today, forever I remain
The Great I am who loves and who saves

Lo, I am with you always forever
I'll leave you never
At night when you close your eyes
I'll lay right beside you
Each day I'll awake you and from the danger
I'll hide you I'm all around you, yet deep inside you

Hope D. Blackwell
Norfolk, VA

Your Hinds' Feet

Father,

I see the mountain goat dangling on the edge of the mountain. You have developed his hinds' feet to be strong and agile. He appears to be so youthful and precarious as he looks over the edge of the great chasm. His continual leaps over the hills and mountain peaks have created hinds' feet that are able to conquer the highest places.

Can You make me like him, my Father? You can show me the way and make me strong like him. I can do all things through Christ who strengthens me (Phil. 4:13). He gives me all I need to overcome all obstacles. This defective world may present only dips and ruts, valleys and storms but Jesus has given me a new name. My new name is written in glory. My new name is "Child of God."

You are the Sovereign Lord, my strength. You have given me hinds' feet to leap on the high places (Hab.3:19). You make me stable and able to stand. You have given me a new heart (2 Cor. 5:17) with high hopes looking to a new home. I trust in You with all my heart, leaning not to my own understanding, in all my ways I acknowledge You and You are directing my path (Prov. 3:5-6). You restore my body and mind. You replace all my doubts and unbelief with faith. I have been made more than a conqueror through You (Rom. 8:37).

You are preparing me for your greatest purpose. Even though my sight is not developed yet to see Your plan, I know You love me and are directing my steps to escalate to the highest levels. You are using my life bringing glory to You here and forevermore. Many are the afflictions of the righteous Dear Lord, and You are my deliverer (Psalm 34:19). You know how to take the extreme situations of defeat as it seemed would take place in Jesus life and You brought such glory out of His. With Jesus strengthening my inner man (Eph. 3:16), He gives me hinds feet to climb upon my high places. There is nothing too difficult for You (Matt.19:26). With You all possibilities transpire to the highest levels of the mountains. I lay aside every encumbrance and run the race before me.

With the love of Jesus,

Julie Chauvin
Katy, TX

Father of lights
Father of colors
Father of us all
Lord, you told us not to be afraid
for you calm our troubled waters
And when the storm is over
A new sign for us is made
up there in the clouds

Everywhere, we see its banner,
its sign of hope
that calms the wrath of water
that brings peace and harmony

In the seven colors up above
we see love form in thy rainbow
It tells us we can HOPE in YOU

Otunuya Okecha
Hyattsville, MD

God's Rainbow

A sign from God,
Sent out of love,
Which shines above
That fleeting flood.

God's rainbow shows
Where His grace flows.
So, look and live!
Pray and believe.

When all is gone,
When dies the fun,
Hope comes at last
To cure the past.

Remember, friends,
That God still cares.
Rainbows, He sends
For all His heirs!

Jerry Jean
Port-au-Prince, Haiti

Words of Encouragement

Trouble doesn't last always, only for a season. A year ago hurricane Frances and Gene destroyed my entire neighborhood; what used to be my home is no longer. God delivered us out of our frustration, anger, hurt, and pain. I know the same God that brought me and my neighbors through will do the same for you. This poem I've written just for you:

Why?

You often ask the question why
When you are hurting deep inside
Looking for answers here and there
In hopes that you would find it somewhere
You toil and toil through the day
And toss and turn throughout the night
And when the morning has finally come
Your eyes are puffed and your limbs are numb

Because you spend all night restlessly
Your body can't function normally
Cheer up my dear this pain will pass
Heartaches and pain never last
A season is all it's allowed to take
This part of life we can't escape
Better days are coming I promise
Look forward to your brighter tomorrow

Tara Ramsey
Deerfield Beach, FL

Dear victims of hurricane Katrina:

Know that God is with you. He knows the broad picture of
our lives that we do not. We need to trust Him and know
that he will be with us in our times of trials and troubles. He
is our refuge and our strength an ever-present help in time of
trouble. We are praying for you and yours. May God our
heavenly Father bless and keep you in his care always.

Patty Freiling
Williamsburg, VA

Dear Jesus! In Your name, I come against all the Katrina devils of doubt, the devils of disgrace, the devils of violence, the
devils of quilt, the devils of fear, the devils of separation, the
devils against job hunting, the devils against house hunting,
the devils against finding relatives. I come against the devils
of unbelief and violence against You.

Dear Jesus! Send Your Spirit into every heart. The hearts which are not open to You, open. You have the control over their minds. Give each child and adult the confidence that You paid for all their sins 2000 years ago. Give them the peace to look forward to eternal presence with You. Make them know that You have a place in heaven with their name on it.

And Dear Jesus! Those who need mothers and fathers and guardians to come back to life, resurrect them from the dead according to Your most gracious mercy. Put life back into their lifeless bodies. And if not, we know You will supply all the needs of every homeless person and every parentless child.

You are the only God of this universe, full of grace and truth.

Rev. Alvin Cordes
St. Louis, MO

What happened here? I don't understand
So much disarray all around me.
I'm sitting here
Alone
Nobody cares

God, where were you? Did you abandon me too?
You told me I could depend on you
You said if I call on your name you'd answer my plea
WELL HERE I AM! I NEED YOU JESUS
I NEED YOU NOW (more than Smokie ever could)

Wait a minute…
Perhaps
In the midst of all this chaos there is something to learn.
Jesus walked on water during a storm
As the water ripped across his face, He didn't slip, fall or lose
his balance.
When the wind tore through his clothes, He didn't lose sight
of his purpose.
He endured.

And no, I am not Jesus.
I am weak, I have my faults.
I cursed my predicament. I blamed my government.
I wondered, Why did this have to happen to me?
God, where is your glory in all of this?

Perhaps, God, you purposed for me to move another
direction.
Maybe, you had something better in store.
I guess I didn't have the strength or faith to step out on my
own, so you did it for me.
"Yeah, that's it."

You said,
"But those who wait upon God get fresh strength.
They spread their wings and soar like eagles" (Isaiah 40:31a
The Message).

I'll never forget my loved ones that perished in the flood.
That engrossing stench of death has forever seared my soul.
And yet, I know I can rise above my circumstance.
I asked myself earlier, "Where is your Glory in all of this?"

Thank you God for your answer,
Now watch me soar.

Anthony Smith
Warren, MI

⌐⌐⌐⌐

Remember how God created you? In His Image and after His likeness He created you, wonderfully and perfectly made. If there was ever a time in your life when you needed to grasp that reality, it is now. Reach within and pull out that spirit part of you that says, "I Am able. Nothing is impossible. With God, all things are possible to him or her who believes . . . that me!

The supernatural, miraculous, and divine are all but a Word away. From this moment on, nothing will pass my lips except words that glorify My God, edify and comfort my fellow man, and bring grace to the hearer. I will lift up the name of Jesus, after all, He died for such an occasion as this. I will speak blessing and Life, not cursing or death. Death is not an option, only Life. I am blessed going in and blessed going out. I am blessed in the city and wherever I put my feet, it will be blessed. Praise God! I have favor with God and I have favor with man. In fact, favor follows me wherever I go. I refuse to go by what my eyes behold. I see Jesus and what He returned back to me, a world of plenty. I see My Father, Who never lies. His Truth is in me.

His love surrounds me; it's gushing out of me. I'm a well spring of Life. From this moment on, I take every thought captive that brings doubt or unbelief, defeat and despair. I think on what is True. God loves me just as much as He loves Jesus. His arm is not shortened that He cannot save. He is waiting for me to agree with Him that all is well . . . I agree and I am waiting to receive from the supernatural, from the very throne of God. His blessings will pour down on me. I'm a child of

His, not forsaken or alone. I am surrounded by Angels that are waiting to assist me. I am surrounded by a great company that have walked before me in this life of faith and had the victory. I am victorious! No plague, will come near me; no harm will overtake me; no weapon formed against me will prosper. I'm victorious! I'm already seated with Jesus Christ and nothing named can exalt itself above the Name of Jesus, my Lord and my Savior. Glory to the King of kings and Lord of lords! Heavenly Father, my ears are open to hear from Heaven.

Holy Spirit, I ask that you lead, guide, and direct me to my new life. Where You lead, I will follow. Whatever you ask or tell me to do, I will do it. I'm willing; I'm ready; and You, Holy Spirit, have made me able. May Jesus Christ's Name be lifted up as I walk this through in obedience and faithfulness to the Word of God. Heavenly Father, I will judge myself daily to make sure I sowed good seeds, words that You provided for me so my harvest is on the way. I receive every good gift You have provided for me and I wait with joy in my heart. The Spirit of God IS up . . . on me to preach the good news, to teach others the Way in which they need to go, to lay hands on the sick and they will recover. The Spirit is working with me to confirm the words that I speak to bring deliverance, healing, and hope. Let the world see Christ in me . . . the Hope of their glory. Amen . . . so let it be written, so let it be done."

Pamela Alexander
Venice, FL

When Jeremiah saw the destruction of his city, home, and people, he cried out to the Lord. In anguish and tears he desperately sought for the comfort that only God can give and he found it. God granted him peace and hope and He will do the same for you as well.

Lamentations 2:9,11; 3:19-20
Her gates have sunk into the ground;
their bars have been broken and destroyed.
Her king and her princes are exiled among the nations,
the law is no more,
and her prophets no longer find
visions from the LORD.
My eyes fail from weeping,
I am in torment within,
my heart is poured out on the ground
because my people are destroyed,
because children and infants faint
in the streets of the city.
They say to their mothers,
"Where is bread and wine?"
as they faint like wounded men
in the streets of the city,
as their lives ebb away
in their mothers' arms.....
I remember my affliction and my wandering,
the bitterness and the gall.
I well remember them,
and my soul is downcast within me.

Lamentations 3:21-26, 55-59
Yet this I call to mind
and therefore I have hope:
Because of the LORD's great love we are not consumed,
for his compassions never fail.
They are new every morning;
great is your faithfulness.
I say to myself, "The LORD is my portion;
therefore I will wait for him."
The LORD is good to those whose hope is in him,
to the one who seeks him;

it is good to wait quietly
for the salvation of the LORD.
I called on your name, O LORD,
from the depths of the pit.
You heard my plea: "Do not close your ears
to my cry for relief."
You came near when I called you,
and you said, "Do not fear."
O Lord, you took up my case;
you redeemed my life.
You have seen, O LORD, the wrong done to me.
Uphold my cause!

In the same way, I have cried out to God for you. I have fasted and mourned for your loss and I know that I am not alone. Many in this great Nation are praying and pulling for you.

But Jesus has stood beside you and said, "I am here. I will never leave you nor forsake you. Trust not in the things of this world, trust only in Me. I will give you My burden which is light and take yours upon My shoulders. I will be with you even until the end of the age. Run to me and I will comfort you. Turn your hearts to Me and I will heal your land."

Never has He broken His promises. It is on this that you can move forward and build your new life. May God bless and keep you.

Edith H. Levy
Glendale, AZ

Dear People - Victims of Katrina!

GOD IS GOOD AND GOD IS LOVE! Nahum 1:7 (The Message) says, "God is good, a hiding place in tough times. He recognizes and welcomes anyone looking for help." The most recognized verse in the New Testament is John 3:16 (New Living Translation) which says, "For God so loved the world that he gave his only Son, so that everyone who believes in him will not perish but have eternal life." Many of us want you to know that God loves you and He hasn't tried to hurt you, kill you, or steal from you. As it says in 1 John 4:8, "God is love," and that love is so all encompassing that He can take even this very bad thing and turn it around for you. The love that was so powerful that He sent His Son so that you could be with Him forever has not stopped - it is still powerful enough to give you victory even now. We are praying for you and I encourage you to TRUST THAT LOVE.

Gloria Hartman
Liberty, MO

⌒⌒⌒ ⌒⌒⌒

Without darkness for the light to shine into, its brilliance might go unnoticed. Please Lord, shine your light into the lives of all our brothers and sisters who so desperately need you now. I pray your loving kindness will cover them, shelter then and strengthen them to hope once again. Show them your hand of loving kindness each and every day as they struggle to begin again. Let them know that they are loved by not only you, but by many who are praying for them daily. In Jesus name I pray and believe. Amen

Nancy A. Molina
Oklahoma City, OK

God and Katrina

If you stood before God right now and there was one question you could ask, what would that be? Some might ask God, "Were you responsible for Hurricane Katrina?" Others might want to know, "Where were you, God, when Katrina was inflicting pain upon us?" Yet others might even dare ask God, "Were you powerful enough to stop the hurricane?"

Natural disasters like Katrina, which strike our comforts, taking away those we love and things we cherish, can either become temptations or tests. Rather than questioning God's goodness and power, it is important to remember our humanity and how much we need God to guide us in times of crises to make the right choices. Equally important, God has given Christians another opportunity to reflect Christ's compassion, care and courage in ministry. As we rebuild our lives and our cities, let us remember God is not weak and God is not wicked; God made the universe with us in mind. It is through the love and care in action from others, especially Christians, that we know God is still present with us and among us. May we also, despite being victims, keep the faith, affirm God's love and reach out to others as well.

Levi C. Williams
Indianapolis, IN

⌒⌒⌒⌒⌒

WHERE ARE YOU, GOD? This is echoed down through the ages....and He is with us all the time! God is not the author of disaster or strife. Rather, He sent Jesus as our intercessor for anything (Philippians 4:6-7) and sends his assigned Angels to guide and direct us through turmoil! God's protection through trials is in writing! (Exodus 23:20-21).

KNOW that ONLY GOOD will rise out of the ruins from

Hurricane Katrina and expect it! Why? Because you have the greatest nation in the whole World (even with our faults or shortcomings) rooting for you and supporting you — either in prayer or supplying your needs as God's extended hand through Christ Jesus! Perhaps this is God's open door for you to have a very, very personal — more than before — relationship with Him....WALKING WITH GOD! It works!

Barbara A. Butler
Reno, NV

The Handprint of God

God, I may not be able to see or touch you, but I feel your presence all around me as I see your heart and your handprint through the love and kindness shown to me by others. When I thought that you had forgotten me—in the midst of darkness and despair, you were there. When I didn't know which way to turn—you were there. Little by little, and day by day, I'm feeling stronger — with a renewed sense of hope. I have the courage to face another day and the faith and the fortitude to rebuild my life. And although I have to sort through the emotional pain of being displaced and of losing it all, something within my soul is telling me to not give up, to rise again.

I will rise this time knowing that my own strength didn't sustain me—but it is you, keeping me alive and that I have a purpose. I survived the storm, so that I could tell others that even in the darkest of night—that you, O God, are there, shining your brightest light—of love, hope, renewal and restoration.

Through the prayers, the love and the support of others, my bowed head is lifted and I can now see beyond the tears and beyond the storm to a brighter future. After the storm, there is always a rainbow to remind us of your loving kindness.

And that is where I will live forever— not in the pain, but

in the promise. I'll live searching for the rainbow and the blessings that you leave behind at the end of every storm. And I won't count what I've lost, but everything that I will gain, both now and throughout eternity, as I trust your hand to lead me to higher ground.

Chiffon French Myricks
Farmington Hills, MI

꜡ᕦ꜡ ꜡ᕤ꜡

It is not easy to understand the design and pattern that God has for our lives. It seems as though life goes in a circle and we cry and we pray to get out of that circle.

Suddenly, disaster hits us and we find ourselves out of the circle, the pattern that we have known, and we wonder if it would have been better if things had remained the way they were. Though it seems now that things are much worse than they were with the same pattern going nowhere, God yet has a plan for your life, "plans of good and not of evil to give you and expected end" and a glorious hope. Out of the desperation he will be there for you. Expect it.

Jeremiah 29:11 (paraphrased)

Elizabeth A. Hairston
Miramar, FL

꜡ᕦ꜡ ꜡ᕤ꜡

What do you say to those who have suffered hardship, misery, and deep sorrow of such magnitude as that hurled upon them by a hurricane named Katrina? The words, "Trust in the Lord" or "He will take care of you"-although they are truth-seem to do little to fill a starving stomach or bring life giving water to parched lips. Angry words of "Why did God let this happen? How could a loving God allow a storm of such death and destruction? Is He bringing punishment and judgment upon us?" Those words rise up in direct conflict with the image of a Father who loves us!

Yet we have seen God's Love displayed in a million ways. Streams of rescuers in boats and helicopters plucking frightened victims from roof tops. Tireless medical personnel treating the sick. Lines of our military passing along cases of food and water into eager hands. Volunteers working long hours in shelters preparing meals and handing out clothes, blankets and toothbrushes. And children holding up hand made signs-"Welcome to our city." Countless little miracles took place not covered by the news media, but ones that will be remembered forever by those touched!

Katrina victims must know there is hope for tomorrow! A Loving Father reminds us of it with the beginning of each new day, and with the promise His Son Jesus Christ left us. "I am the resurrection and the life: he that believeth in me, though he were dead, yet shall he live: And whosoever liveth and believeth in me shall never die. In my Father's house are many mansions: if it were not so, I would have told you. I go to prepare a place for you. John 11:18 and 14:2 KJV Life on earth with its troubles is short term-Heaven is forever!

John and Patty Probst
Authors, *The Last of the Wagon Pioneers*
Whittier, CA

Understanding the plight and devastation of your suffering and frustration is humanly impossible. There are no words to express my heartfelt grief for you. I hope to give you comfort with the same comfort God gives to me in my times of personal trials and tests... "Trust in the Lord with all your heart, and lean not to your own understanding; In all your ways acknowledge Him, and He shall direct your paths" (Proverbs 3:5-6). He is the bridge over troubled waters.

Jeanet R. Broaddus
Bay Shore, NY

⌒℃₰ ₹ᵕ⌒

My prayer for you is that Christ will carry each of you up as a parent carries a child. I remember when I was a child and I was learning how to ride a bike I would ride down the street and sometimes I would fall and get hurt. I remember on one occasion I didn't understand how I fell and all I knew was that I had been hurt. On that occasion my father picked me up and comforted me.

Each of us go through the same situations as I did then and often the pain is much greater; and in these cases we don't understand why these things happen but they do. But know that our Father which is in heaven cares for us and can comfort us; even through these things.

My brother-in-law was in New Orleans at the time of the hurricane, so to all those who survive please know that you are in my prayers.

Sincerely,
John L. Hemphill III

⌒℃₰ ₹ᵕ⌒

In spite of the sorrows that go with tragedies, the great joy that we are assured is in God's Word. "Look, the home of God is now among men, and he will live with them and they will be his people; yes, God himself will be among them. He will wipe away all tears from their eyes, and there shall be no more death, nor sorrow, nor crying, nor pain. All of that has gone forever" (TLB).

God gave this message to John in the Revelation. God loves you and has assured you a place in Heaven for believing in His Son, Jesus, as Lord and Savior. Spending eternity with God will be a glorious new beginning when time here on earth is completed.

Norman C. Bitter, DDS
Fresno, CA

And Jesus taught them, Blessed are the poor in spirit: for theirs is the kingdom of heaven; blessed are they that mourn: for they shall be comforted; blessed are the meek: for they shall inherit the earth; blessed are they which do hunger and thirst after righteousness: for they shall be filled; blessed are the merciful: for they shall obtain mercy; blessed are the pure in heart for they shall see God; blessed are the peacemakers: for they shall be called the children of God; blessed are they which are persecuted for righteousness' sake: for theirs is the kingdom of heaven; blessed are ye when men shall revile you, and persecute you, and shall say all manner of evil against you falsely, for my sake; rejoice and be exceeding glad: for great is your reward in heaven: for so persecuted they the prophets which were before you. Amen!

Charles A. Sykes
Stockholm, ME

All Hope Is Not Lost Yet—There's a Bright Future Still Ahead of You!

Let me start by identifying with YOU (the victim of the recent Hurricane, which is one of the most deadly natural disasters of all times) and to let you know that we are praying for you, and God is with you even in your most trying times as it seems now. The fact that you survived the disaster and are alive today, is the evidence that God has not abandoned you and has plans for your life! He cares and still cares for you. He understands every bit of what you've been through, the loved ones you may have lost, or what you're going through right now. Indeed He is working behind the scene - even without your knowing it. And in time, you'll come to realize that God has been there for you.

You see, the most natural thing to do when one experiences a major disaster which leaves him/her devastated is to want to give up in life. The thought that: "If all I've suffered for all my life can disappear just like that, then what's there for me to live for, hope for or even work for?" Such thought may be expressed in different ways and could result in depression, frustration, discouragement and even accepting defeat. But in all of these, there is still THE GOOD NEWS: THIS IS NOT THE END OF YOUR LIFE! THERE IS STILL HOPE FOR YOU! THERE IS STILL A FUTURE FOR YOU! This book is to encourage you and to let you know that you can still make it despite the devastating setback you've just experienced as a result of the Hurricane's devastation.

However, there is something - a Key - that is very vital to your recovery and to your future success. The devil will want to use your recent experience to rob you of this key that you can't afford to loose as you move ahead in your life, but you'll have a responsibility to guard this key or to recover it if he has already stolen it from you. This Key is: your faith and trust in God and in His ability to restore your life and give you a bright future. Then, to believe in yourself that with God on your side, you can still make it, even more than your past successes put together!

This Key which is expressed in your attitude towards God, yourself and life, is something you'll have to consciously develop during this trying time, and use as an antidote to all the thoughts of depression, discouragement and failure that the devil may often want to fill your mind with.

Let me briefly share with you from the Word of God about some people who had been where you are right now - where they suffered a loss of almost everything they've ever worked or lived for - and how God saw them through and gave them a brighter future than they ever had.

Noah survived the flood and experienced God's blessings: So will you!

"And God blessed Noah and his sons, and said unto them, be fruitful and multiply and replenish the earth" (Genesis 9:1)

After the flood in Genesis 7-8, Noah and his family being the only survivors, God came to him and blessed him. He commanded him to be fruitful, to multiply and to replenish the earth. Despite the loss of everything he suffered during the flood - except for his family - he was still able to multiply and replenish the earth and be fruitful. How did he do it? He was able to replenish everything he had lost to the flood, because of the Blessing of God upon him after the flood. As you learn to put your Faith & Trust in God at this time of your life when it seems you've lost everything, God will put His Blessing on you, and that's ALL you'll need to recover from all your losses. I see God's Blessings come upon you to restore you not to your former position, But to a greater position in life.

David survived the enemy's attacks and later became king: So will you!

"When David and his men came to Ziglag, they found it destroyed by fire and their wives and sons and daughters taken captive. So David and his men wept aloud until they had no strength left to weep...David was greatly distressed because the men were talking of stoning him...But David found strength in the Lord his God...And David inquired of the Lord..." (1 Samuel 30:3-4,6,8).

After David suffered a major attack by the hand of the enemy and lost everything he had. The first thing he did was that he and his men cried until they had no more strength to cry. I guess you've been there. As a result of that, he became distressed. And maybe you've been there too. But after that, he did something that transformed his situation and made him recover all that the enemy stole.

He encouraged himself in the Lord his God and decided to seek God. Consequently, God gave him direction that led to his recovery and ultimately to the Kingship. Now, I believe that you'll recover from your losses, but I also believe that there is "Kingship" waiting for you in your future. Maybe in your career, business, education or talent, I believe there is a star in you waiting to manifest! But you must do exactly what David did.

As you encourage yourself in the Lord your God even as you read this book, I'd want to encourage you to take the next step, and that is to begin to SEEK GOD now for your life. Develop a personal relationship with God and inquire from him what step(s) you need to take at this time of your life, and allow Him to direct your life. I guarantee you that just as David recovered all that he lost and even became King, likewise, I believe God for you that you'll both recover from your losses and even get to the top of your chosen field of endeavor!

Job survived his losses and had twice as much as he had before: So will you!
"Though he slay me, yet will I trust Him..." (Job 13:15).

Finally, I want to call your attention to Job. The man whom we all know so well for the devastating losses he suffered at a point in his life when everything seemed to be going well with him. Yet in it all, it was his faith and trust in God that really saw him through. No wonder he said, "Though he slay me, yet will I trust Him." Your faith and trust in God has to be such that even at a point in your life such as this, you should still be able to say: "Though He slay me, yet will I trust Him." When you have such faith and trust in God in this season of your life, here's what's going to happen to you; It was exactly what happened to Job in his later years, and as you read it, I believe God for you that it'll be your experience too! "And the Lord turned the captivity of Job...Also the Lord gave Job twice as much as he had before...So the Lord blessed the latter end of Job more than his beginning..." (Job: 42:10-12).

I pray the Lord God will bless, encourage and direct you through the message of this book. Amen.

Rev. Vincent N. Paul
Bronx, NY

⌒ ⸜ ⸎ ⸝ ⌒

I cannot pretend to know or fathom the pain you as a victim of this great tragedy are going through, but I know that through it all the Lord's hand is with you and He loves you very much and so do we. Let me share this psalm with you:

"Where can I go from your Spirit? Or where can I flee from your presence? If I ascend into heaven, You are there; If I make my bed in hell, behold, You are there. If I take the wings of the morning, and dwell in the uttermost parts of the sea, even there Your hand shall lead me, and Your right hand shall hold me. If I say, surely the darkness shall fall on me, even the night shall be light about me; Indeed, the darkness shall not hide from You, but the night shines as the day; the darkness and the light are both alike to You. For You formed my inward parts; You covered me in my mother's womb. I will praise You, for I am fearfully and wonderfully made; Marvelous are Your works, and that my soul knows very well" (Psalm 139:7-14).

Know that we are continually praying for your health and prosperity.

Kenneth R. Walls
Bremerton, WA

⌒C⸓ ⸓ↄ⌒

As I sit meditating on what to write, say or whisper to a people that have been through so much and so great a tragedy, I can't help but write what I hear being whispered in the heart of God. New Orleans, New Orleans, this is what the Lord says unto you, who have been bruised and distressed by the strength and might of the wind and water: You are a people I deeply love and long to embrace. I have stretched out my hands to you in this hour, with the love and compassion of a Father. Oh that you would take my hands so that I could walk you into green pastures again.

I will bless this your land. Although I desired to free you from this disaster, but the laws that I set in place are cause and effect related. The only way I could have prevented this disaster is if you would have let me and permit me too. I have given you dominion over the land and I can only access it with your help and invitation. Even as Jeremiah the prophet said, I know the plans I have for you, plans to prosper you and not to harm you, plans to give you a hope and a future.

Take my hand now, and let me walk you into your future that I have prepared for you. Just as the floods rose to a soaring height, so will I cause the trees to sore and to tower once again. I will cause greenery to flourish. The land will once again be pregnant and give birth to the sound of music and laughter, to children playing in the streets, and to increase. Build again and plant again and see my smile on your land, as I restore your home and jobs and lives. You will see an increase like you have never seen before, within the next three years, which is a token of my love. Just as the eyes of all the world have turned upon you to look on you in this time, so too will they hear of the goodness that shall come out of you, the professionals that shall rise out of you and that shall sit even in congress. So lift up your heads and don't be weary, for I am drying your tears with my hand and restoring joy to you as your clothing. Just as a cry of despair came out of you that the world heard, so too shall I raise up voices in you that the world will hear and heed. Voices of Power, fame and renown and people all over the world will rejoice with you, as they have all wept with you.

Robin Rampersad
Orlando, FL

Saved by His Grace to Encourage Others

Beloved children of the most High God, at moments like this, visions may be so blurred with tears that every green light is reconfigured by the mind as red. The next flicker of light at the end of the tunnel may harass the mind as transmitting from an enemy train on a mission for the consummation of the heavenly pillage and plunder. The future may be so gloomy even the mind of the youth may pray it never comes.

But we have a consolation in the indelible word of God. He was true when He declared through the mouth of beloved Apostle Paul: "No temptation has overtaking you except such as is common to man; but God is faithful, who will not allow you to be tempted beyond what you are able, but with the temptation will also make a way of escape, that you may be able to bear it" (1 Corinthians 10:13).

Believe it, dearly beloved, each and every one of you who has survived Hurricane Katrina has been saved by the grace of our most loving God that you may soon be a source of hope to others. And before you know it, you will soon be in the streets, awash with the joy of the Lord, encouraging others.

Charles Anyasi
Lagos, FL

⌒ᴄₑ ₌ᴏ⌒

The strength of the human spirit is amazing! And the strength of the American spirit is more amazing than most. Of the innumerable wonderful things about the United States of America, one of the most wonderful is the indomitable spirit of her people. We are a mixture of people who have deep and abiding faith in the belief that all people are created equal, and we love and hold on to the old adage that "there's no place like home." So to those of you who lost your houses in Hurricane Katrina's wrath, please take heart that you are still "at home" wherever you may find yourselves because you are still in America, our home sweet home.

There is creation in suffering, the Bible assures us of that. And through those who have suffered so greatly will come some amazing and beautiful creative acts of our God. Your suffering is not in vain, for as Isaiah 61:1-4 promises: "The Spirit of the Lord is on [you], because the Lord has anointed [you] to preach good news to the poor. He has sent [you] to bind up the brokenhearted, to proclaim freedom for the captives and release from darkness for the prisoners, to proclaim the year of the Lord's favor and the day of vengeance of our God, to comfort all who mourn, and provide for those who grieve in Zion—to bestow on them a crown of beauty instead of ashes, the oil of gladness instead of mourning, and a garment of praise instead of a spirit of despair. [You] will be called oaks of righteousness, a planting of the Lord for the display of His splendor. [You] will rebuild the ancient ruins and restore the places long devastated; [you] will renew the ruined cities that have been devastated for generations."

Keep a close eye on the places devastated by Katrina; the Lord has big plans for the people of those areas!

Rev. Dr. Barbara Embry
Coaldale, CO

When all was normal, comfortable, and secure, God was there. When all became chaotic, confusing, and unknown, God was there. When fear turns to faith, God will be there. When loss becomes gain, God will be there. When death becomes life, God will be there. When doubt becomes hope, God will be there. The writer of Hebrews says, "Jesus Christ is the same yesterday, today, and forever."

Randy H. Bunyard
Graham, TX

You have been shattered but not broken. You have been hurt but God will heal you. You have been misplaced but God still reserves a place for you. Waters have literally prevailed against you but you have not perished. You are wondering why has God allowed this calamity to uproot your life. I submit to you... Trust in the Lord with all your heart—even though you don't understand his actions and he will deliver you. And that is a promise.

Carla Tibet Oglivie
Dumfries, VA

⌒⸀⸜⸝⸞⸟⌒

"Have I not commanded you? Be strong and coura-geous. Do not be terrified; do not be discouraged, for the LORD your God will be with you wherever you go."

This verse from Joshua 1:9 has long been my favorite. It was the memory verse I taught to my 3rd and 4th grade Sunday school class last Sunday. I told them that whenever they are feeling afraid, all they have to do is quote this verse and remember that God is with them. I told them about how this verse has helped me make it through some of life's toughest storms. I pray that—through the grace of God—this timeless verse from God's Holy Word will do the same for you. God bless you all.

Brittany Miller
Edwardsville, IL

⌒⸀⸜⸝⸞⸟⌒

Somehow when everything seems to be falling apart around us, we need the blessed assurance that comes from the Word of God. God is a lover of us all, and will absolutely never fail us. His strength is perfected in our weakness, and we can always call on His name when we suffer. Psalm 46:1-3 (NIV): "God is our refuge and strength, an ever-present help in trouble. Therefore we will not fear, though the earth give way and the mountains fall into the heart of the sea, though its waters roar and foam and the mountains quake with their surging."

Lord God, please deliver peace in the midst of the storm for all of those who suffer. Give them your peace, which passes all understanding, and comfort them. Bless them and their families along with all those who seek to help them. We ask this in Jesus' name. Amen.

Gerald R. Kaufman
LaGrange, KY

⁓ᴄᵌ⸱ᷱᴐ⁓

The trial that you are experiencing is not the end but the start of a new beginning. Just as a seed that is left on a shelf will remain a seed. But the seed that is buried under the pressure and heat of the ground will be driven to dig deep within to germinate into a much more beautiful and plentiful life. Remember for the child of God, a trial is just an opportunity for God to work in your life. Will you see the trial or will you see the opportunity? It all depends on your faith (Matt. 6:24-34; Rev. 20:19-20; 1 Cor. 3:10-17).

There is a basic difference between a precious stone and gold. Gold is a chemical element, but a precious stone is a compound element. Gold is a chemical element because God created it as gold. But a precious stone has been formed from various kinds of elements, which have been composed together through chemical fusion through countless years of heat and pressure in the earth. Precious stones do not signify something given directly by God, but something which the Holy Spirit has produced in man by much effort and many years of burning. The work of the Holy Spirit on earth is to continually put us into trials so that we may have all kinds of experiences and become precious stones before Him. The precious stones are the product of us being disciplined by Him. The life which God has imparted into us is the gold, while the life which God is constituting in us through His Spirit is the precious stone (Rom. 8:28-29). God is making us in the image of Christ.

Your trials are not meaningless! All true believers have the Spirit of God. But in the ensuing days, God may have put you into certain circumstances to give you experiences in order that you would become chrysolite, chalcedony, sardius or some other precious stone. Each trial causes you to be burned and melted into a new substance, a new precious stone.

Reading a book about precious stones will never cause you to be one—you have to go through the process. The same is true about scriptural knowledge (John 5:39; Matt. 22:29). Without the precious stones the New Jerusalem will never come into existence.

Eric Brown
Missouri City, TX

⌒⌒⌐⌐ ⌐⌐⌐⌐

Our gracious, loving, heavenly Father is in the habit of making your worst nightmare into His greatest, most fabulous dream purposed for your life! How does He do this? I don't know, but He can and He will. If you are able to raise up faith within yourself and exclaim "I believe God is able!"

He promises to be your Shepherd "though you walk through the valley of the shadow of death - [you] will fear no evil." The Son of God can still the storm in your life and give you beauty for ashes, the oil of joy for mourning. True, we weep together in great tragedy and loss. Life springs anew. Choose life and believe your God can truly move mountains for you. Now is the time to summon up the measure of faith within you and cry out in sheer belief. "Make something wonderful out of all this for me, for my family and for my nation. Oh, God I believe You will do it."

Now start looking for things He asks you to be and do; and should He tell you to jump, just cry out: "How high, Lord? How high?" As the years pass and you look back on this horror, I promise your experience of suffering will produce great things. Faith and obedience to God will become your very own treasure and anchor. You get through this time of trouble and you can achieve anything.

Our prayer is for such strength to come to all who have suffered Katrina, whose name means purity. Humanly speaking it is difficult to imagine that you have been brought a "pure blessing" but from heaven's aspect you may well be on the start of "greater blessing."

"My faith looks up to Thee!"

Janice Darline Peipman
Westhampton, NY

The Sparrow

The sparrow, a small feathered thing of very little worth,
So common, who cares, there are millions on the earth.
He's plain, unlike his cousins with yellow, red and blue,
So different from the Goldfinch who boasts its glorious hue.

He's first up in the morning and fills the air with sound,
Not the song of finches, but with chirps he does abound.
He has little going for him – no color, charm or song,
But there is One who cares, One who carries him along.

We often see him dead along the woodland trail,
And show no concern for there are many in the dale.
But God, his Creator, knows each one that falls,
So we, of greater value, He hears us when we call.

Jesus said to His disciples, when on this earth He trod,
"Of more than many sparrows is your value unto God,"
For He has even numbered the hairs upon your head,
So walk in peace and safety, there's nothing you should dread.

So, little sparrow, plain yet bright, I know you're unaware
Of your place in God's Word, and the influence you share;
I'll keep my eyes open as you flit among the trees,
And think of your example when I'm upon my knees.

David T. Peckham
Chelan, WA

Hope's Ebb and Flow

Man's history is written in
      An ever changing tide;
Now base, now noble, then again
      to even baser side.

So in the course of humankind,
      An ebb and flow is found
That washes now to shores sublime,
Then back to depths of ooze and slime
      Where evil does abound.

'Twas when that story first began
      In Eden's garden fair
That man's creator gave to man
The heights of joy, and all that can
Fulfill the righteous heart's demand—
      God's presence with him there.

But on that shore of peace serene
      Man heard the serpent's call
Of pride, and pleasures felt and seen;
And turning from what might have been,
Launched out upon a sea of sin,
Drawn by the ebb into a scene
      Of wickedness—man's fall!

And thus 'twill ever be, it seems;
      The cause of humankind
Is destined in its fickle streams
To flow to shores where noble themes
Inspire and motivate man's dreams,
Where righteous deeds his heart esteems,
And in the love of man, he deems
      Man's purpose is defined;

But lest such noble themes abide,
      And carry man along
To hope's millennium betide,
There is in man a baser side
In which sin's nature does reside,
Which draws mankind with ebbing tide
To depths where goodness men deride,
Where all man's noble thoughts subside
      And evil's grip grows strong.
There, good is evil, evil good;
      There comes no hint of light;
There basest pleasures are pursued,
And right as wrong by man construed;
There blood of innocents they shed
As sacrifice to every mood

Of man who, for convenience, would
Fain hide indulgence 'neath a hood
Of "rights," as if they really stood
      On ground of truth and right.

Then comes a time when men must reap
      The harvest which they've sown.
And for a time of pleasures cheap
Must pay the price, a payment steep,
Of death, despair, destruction deep,
And of regrets which make men weep,
Of freedoms lost while men do sleep
As desolations nearer creep,
Because God's Word they will not keep
      For hard their hearts have grown.

A generation sleeps in dust,
      Barred from the promised land
To forty years of wand'rings just,
Because their God they did not trust;
And for a feast received a crust
Because they cried out in their lust
For Egypt's larders. Now they're lost,
Condemned by God's damnation just
      To desert's arid sand.

How long, how long ere will arise
      A generation new,
Which, purged from evil, now will prize
The things held precious in God's eyes?
Shall forty years see the demise
Of evil's hold and Satan's lies,
And hearts which, turned to Paradise,
      Will righteousness renew?

Thus, ebb returns to flow again,
    And nations seek Thy name.
Thus good men in their strivings win
A victory o'er self and sin

As God and saints their reign begin
And righteousness does direct men,
    For Heaven is their aim.

Yet, ere such flow can ever reach
    Millennium's bright shore,
Mankind must learn what God does teach;
That man's own works God does impeach;
That victory is out of reach
    Without the Spirit's pow'r.

So by each ebbing tide we learn
    Depravity will win,
And hist'ry's lessons each in turn
Assures that men God's laws will spurn,
    Enslaved by self and sin;

Till all men learn to trust the Lord,
    His Holy Spirit claim;
And by God's power, with His Word,
    His sov'reign reign proclaim.

GOD, LET THE HEARTS OF MEN NOW TURN
    TO LIFE AND LOVE AGAIN;
LET RIGHTEOUSNESS FLOW IN RETURN,
    AND FAITH AND HOPE REGAIN.

John C. Brown
Brownwood, TX

❦

Dear God,

I don't understand this situation. I trust in your love and care, your grace and mercy. I know your ways are beyond my comprehension. I may never understand. I have been through enough disasters in my own life and know you are there for me, for us, whether I can take it in or not.

I pray that you would give us the truth, light and wisdom of Jesus Christ. Let us see, sense or hear what you would have us know. I ask that you would take care, as you see fit, of anything seen or unseen that would seek to interfere with your will. I ask this in the strong name of Jesus Christ. Amen.

Kurt-Edouard Neubauer
Dallas, TX

I Will Remember

> Genesis 9:15: "And I will remember my covenant, which is between me and you and every living creature of all flesh; and the waters shall no more become a flood to destroy all flesh."

Have you ever looked up to the sky and seen a rainbow rich with the colors of the spectrum? The first time I recall seeing a rainbow, I was driving and almost had an accident because it was so beautiful. It stretched across the expanse of sky that I imagine measured hundreds of miles.

A friend of mine once told me that he loves to see the rainbow because it reminds him of the covenant God made with us. God promised that He would never destroy this earth by water again. When there are torrential downpours, it is easy to forget the Lord's promise. When floods come and homes are destroyed, remember what the Lord said. Likewise, when the rains of life's trials threaten to destroy us, and we are tempted to give up hope, we must recount these words: "But now thus saith the LORD that created thee, O Jacob, and he that formed thee, O Israel, Fear not: for I have redeemed thee, I have called thee by thy name; thou art mine. When thou passest through the waters, I will be with thee; and through the rivers, they shall not overflow thee: when thou walkest through the fire, thou shalt not be burned; neither shall the flame kindle upon thee" (Isaiah 43:1- 2).

This promise is even more beautiful than the impressive rainbow. More than that, God has made provision for everyone who ever lived on this earth to live in a sin-free world beyond the sky. Jesus is coming in the clouds, and if we are faithful, we will see Him in peace. We who have accepted Jesus Christ will receive the inheritance of Abraham in that day. The beauty of salvation and the covenant signified by the rainbow is that the Lord always keeps His promises. He said that He would look into the sky, see the rainbow, and remember His promise. Since we can see that He is still making good on this promise, we can believe His promise to come again and take us home to live with Him forever in the absolute absence of sin. "Let not your heart be troubled: ye believe in God, believe also in me. In my Father's house are many mansions: if it were not so, I would have told you. I go to prepare a place for you. And if I go and prepare a place for you, I will come again, and receive you unto myself; that where I am, there ye may be also" (John 14:1-3).

L. David Harris (www.knowpeacewithin.com)
Laurel, MD

The Solid Rock

When the storms of life are raging...
And you don't know what to do,
Just put your trust in Jesus...
For He will rescue you.

There is no trial too great,
No matter how big it seems...
That Jesus cannot help you overcome,
As He restores your shattered dreams.

Jesus is the Solid Rock,
Upon whom you can stand,
He alone is the Master...
And He has you in His hands.

Sometimes you may think He's failed you,
When tragedies like the hurricane come...
But believe He is a faithful Savior,
And He will help you overcome.

Though today you may feel sorrow,
And on strange doors you must knock...
Remember Jesus will uphold you,
For He is the Solid Rock.

Mariah Landrum Childs
Winston-Salem, NC

Kind and loving Father, You know it all
Alas! How Katrina afflicted both great and small!
Trials and tears, heartache and pain
Restore your children, dear Lord, from the wound of the
    hurricane
In Thy love and infinite mercy we constantly depend
Nearer, and still nearer to Thee, keep us to the end
Almighty God, for Jesus' sake we ask it all—Our eternal
    Friend!

Michael Pedrin
Karnataka State, India

The day after Hurricane Katrina hit, my devotional reading included Psalm 46:1-2 which says, "God is our refuge and strength, a very present help in trouble, therefore we will not fear, though the earth be moved and the mountains be carried into the midst of the sea." These are words you can hold onto. Your earth has been moved. Perhaps your entire life was carried into the midst of the sea. But God will be your refuge when you feel you have nowhere to go. He will be your strength when you feel you cannot take one more step. He will be your very present help during this time of trouble. He has said he will never leave you or forsake you. Hold tightly to that promise and may you be able to find peace in His comfort and love and strength in the aftermath of this storm. I am praying for you daily, that the Lord will fulfill His promise in Jeremiah 31:13: "For I will turn their mourning to joy, will comfort them, and make them rejoice rather than sorrow." May God's blessings be upon you!

Amy A. Corron
Temperance, MI

Begotten Not Forgotten

Whosoever believes that Jesus is the Christ [Savior] is begotten of God. Whosoever is begotten of God overcomes all obstacles. Who is he that overcomes, but he that believes that Jesus is the Son of God. This is your faith: Know that you are begotten and not forgotten. You shall overcome.

Pastor Phyllis Wiggins
Houston, TX

The Garden

> "Our lives are a fragrance presented by Christ to God....to those who are being saved we are a life-giving perfume" (2 Corinthians 2:15-16a NLT).

In the ever-abiding presence of Jesus is a garden where the fragrance is sweet. There I behold the sweet perfume of His person, inhale the aroma of life everlasting, move in the wind of His grace, and abide in His peace. The beauty of Jesus' garden carries me through the storm and into the calm; its hope is felt throughout the night and renews itself into the day.

When I abide in His garden the fragrance of Christ is carried by the Wind of God by His Holy Spirit; the Wind blows across the places wherein I move and pray.

Lord, make a sweet-smelling garden in the barren places of my life. Let my heart be a garden for Your Spirit. Crush out the weeds. Plant only lovely flowers that bloom and blow sweet fragrance all around it. Plant foliage that sways in the breath of Your Holy Spirit, sending healing to those nearby; a sweet fragrance to You.

Elizabeth B Marshall
Sandy Hook, KY

Oliver Wendell Holmes, Jr. is reported to have said, "If I had a formula for bypassing trouble, I wouldn't pass it around. Wouldn't be doing anybody a favor. Trouble creates a capacity to handle it. I don't say embrace trouble. That's as bad as treating it as an enemy. But I do say, meet it as a friend, for you'll see a lot of it and had better be on speaking terms with it."

How will you come to think of the troubles that have come to you in life. Were they meant to be punishment? Were they random acts without any purpose at all? Will they make you bitter, suspicious, or cause you to be isolated from others for the rest of your life? Perhaps you came through the troubled waters without experiencing loss, perhaps you had nothing to lose. But, many have lost most of what they treasured in life. Now the challenge is to decide how to think about those troubles rather than letting those troubles, those that we cannot change, determine how we live the rest of our lives.

The Apostle Paul teaches us about how to think of troubles in Romans 5, "More than that, we rejoice in our sufferings, knowing that suffering produces endurance, and endurance produces character, and character produces hope, and hope does not put us to shame, because God's love has been poured into our hearts through the Holy Spirit who has been given to us" (ESV vv. 3-5).

When you begin to think that trouble has come and taken away all that you possess, remember that God has planted in the heart of every one of His own a hope that is refined and proved through trouble. Those without that hope will only despair when trouble arrives for they have truly lost everything. Those with hope will be saddened by their losses but they will not despair because nothing in this world can take away everything. There is a well of hope in the heart of every child of God that sees beyond the "now" into the "everlasting" and the hardships of this life only prove to them that their hope is real.

May God bless you as you turn the tragic events of life over in your mind and begin to understand how tragedy clarifies the thinking of a child of God. All that is unessential is melted away to leave a pure and undefiled vessel ready to be used of God. May the words of Romans 8:28 be your comfort, "And we know that for those who love God all things work together for good, for those who are called according to his purpose" (ESV).

Michael Eugene Cannon, Jr.
Spartanburg, SC

⌒ℭ₰ ₷⌒⌒

After natural disasters and other catastrophic events, many people wonder what God is doing. Is God angry at us? Is He asleep on the job? Is there a purpose for this calamity? These are legitimate questions that deserve answers.

The fact is, God exists. He is all-powerful and all-good, but He sometimes allows bad things to happen to accomplish a higher purpose. We will not always understand this purpose. As painful as trials can be, they offer us a wonderful opportunity to trust God. Though I will not pretend to understand the "why" of every event, here are a few reasons why trials sometimes occur:

1. We live in an imperfect world.

2. Evil came into existence because of the gift of free will. Humans have rebelled against God.

God allowed his creatures to choose evil, but did not force them to do so. It has been said that forced love is rape. God will not force His creatures to love Him. Suffering is a bi-product of evil.

3. The reality of suffering gives humans a deeper understanding of goodness in the same way that opposite colors accentuate each other. Sometimes the best way to help someone understand a term is to contrast it with its opposite.

4. God sometimes uses suffering to accomplish a good purpose. Norman Geisler has written, "A drowning person may inspire acts of bravery. . . . God in his providence is able to redeem much (if not all) good out of the evil byproducts in the world." C. S. Lewis wrote that pain is God's "megaphone to rouse a deaf world."

5. Since God is all-knowing, there must be a good reason that He has chosen to allow various disasters to occur. Just because humans cannot always see a reason for evil (or a bad event) does not mean that there is not a good reason. Paul wrote in Romans 11:33, 34: "O the depth of the riches both of the wisdom and knowledge of God! How unsearchable are his judgments and his ways past finding out! For who hath known the mind of the Lord? Or who has been his counselor?" Hebrews 11:3 states that God made the worlds with his word. This is incomprehensible to human understanding, yet it is a basic teaching of Christian theology. Though the Christian faith never contradicts reason, sometimes it goes beyond human ability to understand.

6. It is possible that God could have created a world in which sin or evil would never occur.

However, an all-knowing God chose to allow evil because he knew that this would be the best of all possible worlds—a world in which creatures could choose to love God or to reject God. God must consider a world with free will (with evil as a byproduct) as a better world than one without free will.

The above speculations may help you begin to understand the devastation of hurricane Katrina. Yet, a partial understanding does not necessarily ease the pain you are experiencing right now. Perhaps trusting God in spite of a limited understanding is the most important step you can take. You can take your burdens to Him even now. He wants to bring peace into your life. Meditate on the following words from the New Testament and realize God's peace: "Be anxious for nothing, but in everything by prayer and supplication, with thanksgiving, let your requests be made known unto God; and the peace of God, which surpasses all understanding, will guard your hearts and minds through Christ Jesus" (Philippians 4:6, 7).

Ryan P. Snuffer, D.Min.
Charlotte, NC

There are moments in life that have a way of wounding our hearts; draining away energy, joy, dreams, and to some, even hope. And in that darkness of personal tragedy and despair, we feel all alone, abandoned to the circumstances, as if God Himself has departed our lives. But there is hope, and such an enduring hope! Tragedy can strip away our loved ones, our property, our circle of support; but it can't ever take away God. In the midst of the howling winds of destruction, He was there. As the waters surged and washed away your life, He was there. As you woke up in the midst of a hellish existence, God was there. And though you may not see Him now and feel betrayed by God, He is still there and will forever be by your side through this time of grief. For coming is a day, a very good day in which you will laugh again. You will dream again, and in the process of rebuilding your life, your eyes will be opened to see that through it all, God was there, through the fury of every one of life's storms.

Ubirathan Miranda
Winter Haven, FL

⁓☙ ⁓

As I sit in the comfort and protection of my home, it is easy for me to say, "Just trust God!" Right now, my world is far away from your devastation. However, I want you to know I am coming to you with a group of men to stand with you. I am the one who will hand you that bottle of water; lift your pet to safety; cuddle your crying child and wipe their tears; stand beside you in silence because I cannot think of an appropriate word to say. We will dig in the rubble and help make your life new. We can never make it the way it was; but maybe we can make it better than what it is right now.

Even if you cannot trust God right now, can you find it in your soul to trust us? I pray you can. We desire to be flesh for God to wear until you can begin to have confidence in Him again. A man named Philip Yancey wrote, "Trust does not eliminate the bad things that may happen... Trust simply finds a new outlet for anxiety and a new grounding for confidence...." We will not remove the bad things of yesterday, but maybe our presence will help bring a renewed confidence for tomorrow. In that confidence you will find God, and when you find Him, you will see His grace surrounding your life.

I have always been told that we should never doubt in our darkness what we knew in the light. The darkness of your surroundings has changed your world - forever. But remember, there was a time when you truly believed, "The God who adds a little dewdrop upon the flower in the morning is the same God who put the stars in place and designed the path of every constellation in the heavens. And if Jehovah can care for all that, then surely He can care for me..." (A. Redpath).

He is near. He has never left you, and He cares... deeply!

Ron Sears
New Castle, DE

⁀ᴄ₊ ₴ᴑ⁀

I had a brother who lost his house in 1999 to Hurricane Floyd. He and his family lost everything. However, as time has passed, God has been faithful and they have been able to put their lives back together, with God's help; you will as well. An encouraging word from God for times such as this is found in Isaiah 43:1-4 (New Living Translation): "But now, O Jacob, listen to the Lord who created you. O Israel, the one who formed you says, 'Do not be afraid, for I have ransomed you.

I have called you by name; you are mine. When you go through deep waters, I will be with you. When you go through rivers of difficulty, you will not drown. When you walk through the fire of oppression, you will not be burned up; the flames will not consume you. For I am the Lord, your God, the Holy One of Israel, your Savior... Others were given in exchange for you. I traded their lives for yours because you are precious to me. You are honored, and I love you.'" In spite of the loss and pain that you are experiencing, remember that God is with you during this very difficult time. Our prayers are with you as well, asking for His help, direction and strength.

Roland E. Cavanaugh
Thomasville, NC

⁀ᴄ₊ ₴ᴑ⁀

Our hearts grieve as we see our brothers and sisters suffer from this devastation of nature. Our prayer for you is that you will find peace and hope from God during this time of turmoil. A verse of Scripture that has helped me during such times of upheaval in my life is found in Isaiah 40:31: "But those who hope in the Lord will renew their strength...they will soar on wings like eagles, they will run and not grow weary, they will walk and not be faint. May the God of hope be with you at this time; may you find inner peace as you put your trust in Him."

David E. Miller, Ph.D., Psychologist
Reynoldsburg, OH

Everything you cherish is gone; all the nice things people could say are now meaningless. Any words that could contain hope have now become empty. If you want to curse God and die no one could blame you.

All that I can offer you is that I will commit to pray for you! Hang on there has to be some reason for you to do so.

Mark I Sharp
Warsaw, IN

Valleys at times represent the low times of our lives. Valleys also come in different shades and forms. What has happened to you is not only a valley in your life, but in the life of this nation. However, we are not to fret in the valleys that befall us, because God our creator said "though you walk through the valley of the shadow of death, you shall fear no evil, because, He is with us and His rod and staff comfort us. Saints, please know that even in this valley, His rod and staff comfort you. And even this situation will work together for

your good and the good of your family.
    Cast your burden on Him and He will take care of you.

William Femi Awodele
Omaha, NE

Hope

Beacon in the bleakness,
Lighthouse in the night:
We see that radiant brightness
To guide us through the fight.

Though darkness might surround us
With pain and shock and fear,
Yet we walk with courage
For we know that God is near.

America has weathered
Many storms as fierce:
As civil wars and trials
Choose our hearts to pierce.

But America the beautiful,
One nation under God,
Shall rise again in glory
Upon this holy sod.

We hope and pray for God's blessings upon His children at
this time.

S. Megan Payne
Falcon, CO

Your Promises Are True

Dear Lord,
Your promises are true. They never fail.
You promised never to leave nor forsake us
And when Katrina struck with all her might
And our forts were too weak for her gusts,
You were there.

When she birthed torrents of rain
Turning cities into ponds overnight,
You were there.

When our bones grew frail from fear
As families and friends were torn apart
You were there.

You promised to deliver us from trouble
And as the waters rose all around us
Drowning our hedges, havens, and homes
You made a way through our sea
And led us safely to dry ground.

You promised all things, without exception,
Would work together for our good.
Thank you for using Katrina to give us a new beginning.
You have preserved our lives for a purpose
And will replenish all that we've lost.
Our future will be better than our past.

Thank you for the promise of eternity in heaven,
For those who lost their lives in the wake of Katrina
Shall awake in glory never to lose it again!

Peter Adebi
Blackwood, NJ

⁓᷿᷿᷿⁓

Precious one:

Today, find a resting place in the arms of Jesus. He is your answer, there is no other place to turn. He is the arms you need to embrace you right now. He wipes every tear from your eyes and hears your cry. He's closer to you right now than anyone that has or will ever be near and dear to you in this life. He is the Lover of your soul; He created you for His glory and pleasure.

Today, precious one, is a brand new life for you. He washes the pain, fear and tragedy away with His all-encompassing LOVE. Holy Spirit, breathe the breath of life into this precious one today. Embrace them and nestle them in Your arms. As they read these simple words, Holy Spirit, let the fire of Your loving power overtake them now flooding peace to their souls, hearts and minds. Let Your all-consuming fire burn up all things that would hinder their new life in You.

May the Lord bless you and keep you, may the Lord make His face to shine upon you and be gracious to you. May the Lord lift up His countenance upon you and grant you peace.

My prayers are ever flowing for you today.

Sister Dolores Tansil
Grand Blanc, MI

⁓᷿᷿᷿⁓

I am confident that New Orleans will be rebuilt, and that the rich tradition of this city will live on. That this will be one more ballad in New Orleans' rich history. I have the image that even as we speak, some famous jazz legend, held up in some relief shelter, is already writing on a scrap of paper, using Hurricane Katrina as an opportunity to write the next great blues ballad—a ballad that would be remembered for generations to come.

You are in my prayers. Peace be with you.

Daniel Salomon
Newton Centre, MA

Prayer for Connections

Father God, You are a God of divine connections. Even though I have been displaced, I ask You to connect me with those people and those things that I need and that You want in my life. I thank You for direction every day when I awake and even when I sleep. I thank You for a new life, a life directed by You. Father, Your Word says in Psalm 68:6 (Amplified translation) that You place "…the solitary in families and…" that You give "the desolate a home in which to dwell." Father, I thank You for connecting me with my displaced family members and I thank You for giving us a home in which to dwell. I thank You for giving me a new job, a new church, and new friends. I thank You for bringing my family to a greater knowing of Your love and mercy. Help me to extend Your love and Your mercy to others who cross my pathway. Thank You, Father, for working out this situation and causing it to turn for my good. You are a good God and I praise Your name. I expect those divine connections to manifest in my life minute by minute. In the name of Jesus, I pray. Amen.

Carolyn B. Anderson
Douglasville, GA

We Hope Therefore We Cope

The mystery of calamity continues. I hate to admit it, and it is definitely not prophesying doom, but Katrina tragedy is not the last of the catastrophes that mankind will witness. The question, therefore, is not "Will something like this happen again?" The question, however, is, "When, where, what kind and who will be the victim?" Since we don't have answers to any of the components of this question, it is the reason we cannot appropriately plan strategies against such tragedies.

Does it mean that there is nothing we can do at all? No! There are things to be done. We may not stop the tragedies but we can check our foundation. I am not talking about the foundation of an earthly building. I am talking about the foundation of our life.

Though many people cannot resist the temptation to stipulate reasons for such things, the fact is that in most of the cases these are but speculations that help very little, if any. When a tragedy strikes, people usually respond by blaming one another, the leaders, the government and God. Again, passing of blame in this manner doesn't help anything.

Here we are and tragedies are part of our experience, what do we do? What is important is the foundation of our life and how we balance the present against the eternity in proportions to how we perceive their value. The Bible records in Romans 5:1-5 (NIV): "Therefore, since we have been justified through faith, we have peace with God through our Lord Jesus Christ, through whom we have gained access by faith into this grace in which we now stand. And we rejoice in the hope of the glory of God. Not only so, but we also rejoice in our sufferings, because we know that suffering produces perseverance; perseverance, character; and character, hope. And hope does not disappoint us, because God has poured out his love into our hearts by the Holy Spirit, whom he has given us".

In tragedies, some people perish as others remain to lament

the losses (see Luke 13:1-5). The portion of Romans 5 we have quoted above shows us the path of survival. It is not an easy one, but the only one. We start with rejoicing in the HOPE of the glory of God (v.2b). This hope gives us the possibility to step onto the supernatural platform where we can "rejoice in our sufferings." If this happens, then calamity will not weaken but strengthen us. The path is therefore in this wise: Rejoicing in the hope of the glory of G — rejoicing in suffering — trained in perseverance — formation of an enduring character — grasping of the hope that never disappoints. Hope that does not disappoint is the hope that is "fully baked" and "rightly focused."

It is only if we have the hope that doesn't disappoint that we would be in a position to "manage" suffering. Suffering is here to stay, we have no choice but to arm ourselves to manage it. The best way of managing suffering is to rejoice in it. I know this doesn't sound compassionate to tell someone who has lost everything including loved ones. But what other options do we have for survival? I must say that faith is a fight (1 Tim. 6:12, 2 Tim. 4:7).

But what does the Bible mean by saying that hope doesn't disappoint (Rom. 5:5)? In reality, there are many people who have hoped for certain things without getting them. Were they disappointed? Maybe, but this is only if they minimized the scope of their hope. We read in 1 Corinthians 15:15 (NIV): "If only for this life we have hope in Christ, we are to be pitied more than all men." Yes, we can hope in Christ for this life but it doesn't end there. If hoping in Christ only for this life is a pity, what can we say about those who hope for welfare in this life without acknowledging Christ at all?

In 1 Corinthians 13, hope is counted among the three things that shall not pass away: "And now these three remain: faith, hope and love. But the greatest of these is love" (v. 13, NIV). If our hope is grounded on Christ, it means that even when one has lost all things, including life itself, his loss is not ultimate if his hope was set at the right place. We need hope to keep our faith and we need faith to keep our hope. Hebrews 11verse 13 and 39, tells us something about faith that implies the reciprocal relationship between faith and hope. This brand is rarely preached: "All these people were still living by faith when they died. They did not receive the things promised; they only saw them and welcomed them from a distance. And they admitted that they were aliens and strangers on earth…These were all commended for their faith, yet none of them received what had been promised" (NIV).

Dear beloved ones, if we capture the scope of our hope, we shall cope in every trying moment while we sojourn on this side of life. Remember, the three—faith, hope and love—endure forever. This is how they endure: Faith that counts is when you have all reasons in place to doubt God, yet you stubbornly choose to trust Him who reigns in eternity; Hope that counts is when things are hopeless yet you choose to count on God for whom all things are possible. If it didn't materialize here, then God plans to "compensate" for it in eternity; Love that counts is maintaining your affection for God even when He seems to have "failed" you. The truth is that God's love endures forever. That means that death or loss of all things doesn't mean that He has forsaken you.

For people who don't have a relationship with Christ, perhaps this is the time when you are bitterly asking, "If there is an almighty, compassionate and loving God, where was He when Katrina hit?" There is something mysterious about God that we will never understand on this side of life. This mystery doesn't include the consideration that He doesn't exist. An element of this mystery is also innate in man. Isn't it puzzling that we wonder why godless people who have had things going their way most of their life are generally bound to complain more bitterly against God when such calamities hit than people who believe in Him? Maybe God is telling us that those things that we build our life around can go in no time. God may be telling us, "It is not necessarily because you are 'good' that you are living and having it all going for you." Equally, it is not necessarily because someone is wicked that he dies (see Luke 13:1-5). Whether we live or die, life is a mystery that only God knows how He manages it. Maybe God is calling our attention away from the material world—and this is not only for the unbelievers but even us Christians.

I pray that the Lord Himself will comfort you and assure you that faith, hope and love live. May the Lord use this destruction for the construction of hope that defies calamity; may He use this tragedy to help us become better rather than bitter.

Daniel Owino Ogweno
Skien, Norway

He Hears

The Lord of the skies can hear your crying
He feels your pain and knows your sighing
He stretches his loving hands to you
And He understands your anger too

He's only a whispered prayer away
He'll bring back color when skies are grey
He knows the pain that you are feeling
He wants to bring today His healing

So won't you come and sit by His side
And know the peace that He'll provide
To those who seek his awesome love
For they'll find mercy from heaven above

Ned Jacob Haddad
Scarborough, Ontario

Walk on Water

Tossed and blown upon the water,
Till I cried out Jesus' name.
Since that day of my salvation,
I have never been the same.

Walk on water. He'll uphold me
With His mighty, loving hand.
And my faith it will not falter,
For I know by me He'll stand.

Now my days are filled with gladness,
As I serve my loving Lord.
For I know that when I leave here,
He has promised my reward.

Walk on water. He'll uphold me
With His mighty, loving hand.
And my faith it will not falter,
For I know by me He'll stand.

Linda Machado
Meriden, CT
Copyright © 2005 by Linda Machado

⌒⌒⌒

Many "Christians" have risen up and said that "God did this"
or that "God is judging you" by sending this massive hurricane
that destroyed your homes and even taken the lives of many.
For this I want to say "I'm sorry." The God that I serve brings
only life and liberty, not death and destruction. I say to you
this day "it was not God." God doesn't have hurricanes to give!
He loves you with an everlasting love. The Bible says that God

poured all His anger and wrath out on Jesus. All means all! He is not mad at you and He's not judging you. In Christ, there is hope and there is healing for you heart. Jeremiah 29:11 says that God has a good plan for your life! We are praying for you and we are sending support to back up those prayers. Remember that God is a good god and He loves you so much!

Tammy L Dahl
Eustis, FL

Peace is not the absence of storms, but inner serenity in the face of storms
Courage is not the absence of fear, it is fear that has said its prayer
Joy is not the absence of problems, it is an inner spring gushing out regardless of problems
Be still, dear one, and find comfort in God
Though you may not feel Him, He is here, right here with you.
Lovingly He is saying, "Smile, dear child, this storm will pass"

Akinwale Akindiya
Lagos, Nigeria

A Staying Hand

Dark was the color of the day as the wind's invisibility roared like a thousand trains rushing uncontrollably to an unknown destination. The rains plummeted as if all of God's angels were exhaling in unison as heaven's fountains flowed unabated. The marauding water stalked every entry, flinging death and destruction about as it angrily searched for uncharted ground.

Twisted metal, mixed with wood and steel, created an eerie landscape as lonely roofs and precious keepsakes punctuated the liquid surface. But a staying Hand was in control of the slicing winds, the slashing rains and the destiny of all. God is calm…God is in control!

We are told in Psalm 24:1 that "The earth is the Lord's and the fullness thereof; the world, and they that dwell therein." As difficult as it may seem at this time, God is ever present and always in control of every single event that occurs in each of our lives, regardless of its severity! After all, God is the Divine Creator. Billions and billions of stars He set into the universe (Genesis 22:17). He spoke into existence the various planets (Hebrews 1:2); He set the winds circular motion (Ecclesiastes 1:6) and charted the ocean currents (Psalms 8:8).

God has complete control over all of nature. Yet, hurricanes rage, waters rise and tornadoes devastate. Why? Perhaps it is to allow us a tiny peek at the sovereignty of God. Only He can stem the tides, hold back the storms and control the weather. In Luke 8:22-25 we read of Jesus calming a storm. In this account we see that Jesus and some men were sailing when a fierce wind arose and the boat began taking on water. The men were extremely frightened and feared for their lives. As this storm raged, Jesus slept. Upon being awakened by the terrified men, Jesus rebuked the wind and the raging waters, and calm descended upon the water. Then He asked a very important, perhaps the most important question of anyone's life, "Where is your faith?"

Katrina was a devastating blow, a horrific and heartbreaking catastrophe that has rocked our country. Lives have been lost, families torn apart, homes nothing but a pile of rubble. Sadness, fear and uncertainty live in the minds of thousands as the grim reality of picking-up the pieces and moving forward lay ahead. Only faith and trust in Jesus Christ, who is the author and finisher of our faith, can again bring us joy and hope for the future. Place your trust squarely on Him, and even though hardships are presently overwhelming, He will see you through!

"Looking unto Jesus the author and finisher of our faith; who for the joy that was set before him endured the cross, despising the shame, and is set down at the right hand of the throne of God" (Hebrews 12:2).

Nancy Hamilton
Marietta, OH

⌐⌐⌐

Colossians 1:16-17 (AMP) says, "For it is in Him that all things were created, in heaven and on earth, things seen and things unseen, whether thrones, dominions, rulers or authorities; all things were created and exist through Him (by His service, intervention) and in and for Him. 17 And He Himself existed before all things and in Him all things consist - cohere, are held together."

Isn't it wonderful to know that Jesus Christ, the creator and maintainer of the universe, does care about us? Why He cares so much for us that He said every hair on our heads is numbered!

Isn't it awesome to know that not one bird falls to the ground without His knowledge and yet He tells us we are of more value to Him than that bird?

Isn't it comforting to know that if we seek Jesus' kingdom first and not worry about the material things of life that He will provide all our needs because we are of greater value than the flowers and the birds which He created and sustains?

Isn't it reassuring to know that Jesus is our brother and is ready to carry our loads when they are far too heavy for us?

But most encouraging of all is to know that such personal

attention is guaranteed by the One who created and maintains every atom in the universe? Yes, that's right, the very same One!

Robert Chapman
Perth, Western Australia

With Everlasting Love!

With Everlasting love I have treasured you and will share with you joy that has no end. I've longed forever to talk with you face-to-face, friend-to-friend I know your sorrows I've felt each and every blow I took your place at Calvary that my love for you would show

I know the world has tried to separate us with every style and trend The enemy of your soul has tried to defeat you with strong tides and every adverse wind I know how confused you were, with all his devilish charms Yet you have held tight to your hope in God's everlasting arms

Take courage; be strong, when pain and sorrow seem to have no end I know the course you take, I have been there with you for all the brokenness to mend With everlasting love I have treasured you; and to give you joy that will never, ever end This my word I promise, spoken not to my servant; but as friend to friend

You are my treasured possession from all eternity past The treasures of the world are temporal but the gift of God will last and last With everlasting love I treasure you, all your ways will mend You'll have peace with God and joy and happiness that will never ever end.

George E Woodards
Evanston, IL
© George Woodards
August 14, 2004

"I will lift up mine eyes unto the hills from whence cometh my help. My help cometh from the Lord which made heaven and earth" (Ps. 121:1-2).

As a native of Louisiana with relatives in Mississippi and Alabama I write these words of comfort to my brothers and sisters who are courageous survivors. In moments like these, it is important to face in the right direction.

1. First, it is important not to spend too much time speculating about what the future may bring. Right now your job is to try to focus on the future and not be consumed with the past. It is very difficult to drive forward effectively while looking in the rear view mirror. Taking one day at a time, could be good counsel during a time like now. Sometimes we have to trust God even when we can't trace him. God already knows what the future holds, right now live in today and trust him with the tomorrows.

2. Prioritize what you are counting. Perspective is important in moments like these. Are you looking at what you have or don't have. To have life is a wonderful gift to begin with. Hank Aaron hit 755 homeruns and struck out more than 1,000 times. We celebrate him as the homerun king. We could also give him a trophy for strikeouts. It all depends on what you are counting. Someone once said they spent an entire day complaining about their feet hurting until they saw someone with no feet at all. Find, celebrate, and count as many positive things you can find in and around you.

3. Lift up your eyes and look in front of you. That's where All of your future is. I once heard someone say, "If life ever knocks you down, try to land on your back. Because if you can look up, you can get up" (I believe you can and will get up). If our help comes from the Lord (and it does) it might be a good idea to lift up your eyes unto the hills. That is, in

fact, where all of our help comes from.

Blessings,
Dr. Charles Phillips
Washington, DC

꜒ᘁᱽᱽᘁ꜒

Even in the aftermath of the most devastating circumstances, like a hurricane or volcano, God can create beauty. Just as he put a rainbow in the sky after the flood as a sign for us in Noah's day, so too will he bless you with signs that his promises are eternal. I pray that you will seek him and let him guide you as you recover from this devastation. He is faithful and will always answer those who seek him.

Mary Christine Moore
Lawrenceville, GA

꜒ᘁᱽᱽᘁ꜒

When your life's going down and you're feeling all alone,
When you're stressed and depressed, feeling weary and dis-
    owned,
When your pain is overtaken with a heartache and despair,
And you look all around you and you think that no one cares.
Just remember God still loves you and He'll be there 'cause He
    cares.
He never leaves you nor forsakes you, He is just and He is fair;
All He wants is you to love Him as He you beyond compare.
He's the key, unlocks your treasure, the one that's there, the
    one that's rare.
Just call out to the name of Jesus and you'll see your future
    change.
Father, Son and Holy Spirit, your life will never be the same.

I speak because I have experienced the things I speak are things
    I lived,
Was it not for the love of Jesus,
Freely I received and freely I will give.

Lou Acosta
Lorain, OH

                                   ⌒ ⌒

"They that sow in tears shall reap in joy" (Psalm 126:5).

Dear loving heavenly Father, only You can turn such tragedy into blessing. Please lead many to put their hope and trust only in You, and in Your great mercy and grace, encourage and sustain Your children. May the joy of Your blessings comfort all those who have suffered, and draw all in our country to humble themselves before You, that You may revive and heal our nation. Amen.

Rory Roybal
San Jose, CA

What Can I Say Today?

What will I say at the end of the day,
When everything dear to me has been washed away?
Some would tell me just curse God and die,
But then, how would I face Him in that world beyond the sky.

I know what I am going to say today!
I am going to praise Him for this new way!
I am going to thank my Father above
For His enduring Love!

I know what I am going to say today!
I am going to say to my Heavenly Father, if I may,
Thank you for Jesus who died for me,
That through His grace I am set free.

Free to call upon my God and Friend.
Free to accept His forgiveness of my sin.
Free to sing His joyful song.
Free to trust Him to right this wrong.

Howard Eugene Wright
Yates Center, KS

The power of healing is not found in the question of why as much as it is found in the answer of who. It is the trials of mankind that brings a perspective that causes us to stop, and think about eternal things. In whom is the answer of eternity? His name is Jesus! It is these times, when all seems stripped away that we realize that naked we came into the world, and naked we shall leave it. In that understanding we realize that our real only hope, love, and only salvation, when all else falls, is the one who gave it all on the cross for us. That one is Jesus, and he is alive for you in your time of need.

Rev. David M. Berman
Richmond, NH

Pick Up a Cross

Katrina slammed into the coast,
An act of God or was it?
A path of destruction left behind,
Like a bull in a china closet.

Thousands dead and thousands homeless,
Cities lay in ruin.
An act of nature or evil force,
Or was it all God's doing?

I asked these questions for many years.
And learned the reason could matter less.
I'm now too busy in God's vineyard,
Caring for my wife who has MS.

Katrina provided a half million reasons,
That make it plain to see.
Why Jesus said to one and all,
Pick up a cross and follow me.

Ethan W. Moses
Madison, AL

My name is Allen Styles and my prayer goes out to all those who have been affected by Hurricane Katrina. I also pray that you will be encouraged by these scriptures from God's word.

> God is our refuge and strength, an ever present help in trouble. Therefore we will not fear, though the earth give way and the mountains fall into the heart of the sea, though it's waters roar and foam and the moun-

tains quake with their surging (Psalm 46:1-3).

The Lord is close to the brokenhearted and saves those who are crushed in spirit (Psalm 34:18).

I sought the Lord, and he answered me; he delivered me from all my fears (Psalm 34:4).

He (God) heals the brokenhearted and binds up their wounds (Psalm 147:3).

Though, things seems dim at this time, I encourage you to trust in the Lord with all your heart and lean not on your own understanding; in all your ways acknowledge him and he will direct your path (Proverbs 3:5-6).

God loves you and so do I. Again, my prayers are with you all.

Allen Styles
Tucker, GA

Hope in God's Rainbow

There's a rainbow in the sky
you may not see
There's a rainbow in the sky
for you and for me
There's a rainbow in the sky
and guardian angels too
dispatched to bring you hope
and watching over you
So don't give up
no matter how hard things get for you

Just remember,
There's a rainbow in the sky
and in my heart
for you.

(Psalm 30:5; Psalm 91:11-12)

Barbara Jean Carr
Richmond, CA

❦

Some of the worst things that ever happened to me in life have also been some of the best. Now you might wonder what I mean, how can something bad end up good? I am not sure how it happens, but there is a transformation that occurs. It happens during the dark nights when worry seems to overtake every thought and sleep seems impossible. In the midst of this dark night there comes a little tiny hope. It is like a little candle on the darkest night. It comes forth in a word, or thought; it is that "good" thought in the midst of all the bad ones. It happens when thanksgiving penetrates the midst of the storm.

I was once homeless. I had a newborn baby and a 4-year-old daughter. It was very hot and we had no home. Some friends gave us an old travel trailer that had one room. My husband made some beds with donated wood, and we put air mattresses on the wood. We set up a tarp outside in the front for our kitchen, and put up a curtain outside on the back for our bathroom and used a little porta-potty. We had a garden hose and washtub for our sink. It was horrible and I complained every minute of the day. It was so hot and the place where we camped had blackberry thorns everywhere... not much fun for a 4-year-old. I was kept busy keeping her contained so she didn't get hurt by the thorns. I moaned and groaned at our plight. Whenever we went anywhere I would look at people's homes along the way and envy them. If I saw a big house that was partially empty, I would complain that it wasn't fair, those people had too much and I had too little.

After a month or so of this kind of living I awoke early one morning and went outside to our makeshift kitchen. It was a beautiful morning, the kind where birds are singing and the air smells fresh and clean. I started to think all the negative thoughts that I had thought each day, but something in me said "try giving thanks instead." Now, you might wonder what in the world I had to give thanks for, living in that horrid situation. But, as I sat there enjoying the morning, I began to go through the mental list. I had my baby and she was healthy. I had my health. I had food and shelter. I had love in my life. I had God! So, as I began to give thanks in that place, the bitterness in my heart lifted. I felt so much better. I started cooking a wonderful breakfast for my family in that makeshift kitchen. My thankful heart was a balm to my entire family that morning. In fact, whenever I think of the good things I have enjoyed during my life, that scene is one of my best memories.

Within days of that "thankful" event, our lives changed. A job, housing, all our needs were met. God provided so abundantly. But I will never forget the morning or the wonderful worship that ensued, the day I gave thanks in the midst of trial. It was one of the best days of my life.

Since that time I have been through many good times and many bad times. But in the midst of them I have learned to look for the hidden blessings and give thanks for them. Having a thankful heart truly is a good medicine!

Lori K Hankins
Moravian Falls, NC

A storm puts you in a position in life at which things around you become uncomfortable and contrary to your destination and your faith. Faith is a deep conviction of internal belief that produces corresponding action. Faith works from the inside out, not the outside in. Faith is based on promises not a problem. Because you walk by faith and not by sight, this is really no major problem at all. It may look bleak and brim but God is in control.

Always know that there are different kinds of storms. There are storms of correction. There are storms of direction, and then there are storms of perfection. You should know that God knows how to provide you a way of escape. You still have a destination that God is taking you to. You need to know that according to Romans 8:28 it says, "All things are working together for the good of them that love him, and those who have been called according to his purpose. It will work out for your good. Your destination is fulfilling His purpose. This was a storm of direction and perfection. Your direction has changed, but your perfection has begun. He who begins a good work in you will see it through until it has been completed.

C. Regi Rodgers
Las Vegas, NV

Raising UP

I sit alone hungry and cold
Under the bleaching brightness
Of New Orleans sun.
The glam and glit gone.
The wind forgotten
The roar of those dying
A thousand deaths
Before the flames of forgotten breath.

I watch helplessly.

Dreams of necessities not there
Wishing for rain to wash,
To cool,
To drink.
Taunted by liquid death
Of waves possessed.

Desperate and drab.
Stop the insanity on the TV
Just a minute to help me
Lift my sunken shadow
Lost in thoughts of things past
No longer there
All that's left is life's despair.
And God.

BUT GOD.

I look up
I reach up
I get up
Before myself
Besides myself
And beyond myself
To capture your strength
Within me
That others may see
Your light.

There's no purpose here unless it's that you might
Be glorified.

It hurts to think
But I cry
I sigh
And then, I try.

"… My grace is sufficient for thee: for my strength is made perfect in weakness. Most gladly therefore will I rather glory in my infirmities, that the power of Christ may rest upon me" (2 Corinthians 12:9, KJV).

Kedra A. Dumas
Dallas, TX
© Copyright 2005, Kedra A. Dumas

…and He said:
Blessed are the poor in spirit, for theirs is the realm of heaven.
Blessed are the mourners, for they will be comforted.
Blessed are the humble, for they will inherit the earth!
Blessed are they that hunger and thirst for what is right, for they will be satisfied.
Blessed are the merciful, for upon them will be mercy.
Blessed are the pure in their hearts, for they will behold God!
Blessed are the peacemakers, for they will be called sons of God.

Translation from the Aramaic Gospel of Matthew—dedicated to all those we pray for.

Joseph Pashka
Quincy, IL

God's Word

I searched the Word for "hope" in a time of chaos and confusion;
   I found it.
I searched the Word for "love" in a world of hate and violence;
   I found it.
I searched the Word for "comfort" in a time of grief and
   sorrow; I found it.
I searched the Word for "truth" in the midst of great deception;
   I found it.
I searched the Word for "salvation" knowing it was what I
   needed; I found it.

To the hurricane victims; may you find comfort and help in
the Word of God and may you regain your lives once again
through the support and love of a caring world. God bless you
as you begin again, rebuilding your lives and homes, with a
greater strength and determination from what you have been
through. My prayers are with you!

Mary Hope Henley
Greenwood, AR

When the winds and storms of life seem to over take us,
know that God has a plan for your life. His plan is to prosper
you and not to harm you to give you a hope and a future.
Despite what it looks like right now in the midst of the devastation you can be assured that God has already worked out
your situation. He is already supplying all your needs. Take
this time to give thanks for your very life. He said weeping may
endure for a night but joy comes in the morning light. Be still
and know that He is God and He is not willing that any would
perish but all would come to the full knowledge of the truth.

The truth is no weapon formed against you can prosper and all things work together for the good of those who love God and are called according to His purpose.

Like Paul, I being a war veteran know I can be content in whatever state I'm in because God will never leave me nor forsake me, and you too can take comfort in that very same truth. Remember He said He would keep you in perfect peace if you keep your mind stayed on Him, knowing that He is a rewarder of those who diligently seek Him. My prayers and those of countless others are with you because we know that the prayers of the righteous avail much and what the enemy meant for bad God will make good. This is a time to place your total trust in God, the author and the finisher of your faith. So be encouraged, keep the faith, and when you've done all you can do to stand, then stand. Let the joy of the Lord be your strength. Let your light shine that others will see and know that there is a God and He lives in you and in that you have hope. Let your hope, strength and fortitude be a testimony and a blessing for those around you.

I am reminded of 2 Corinthians 12:9 (Amp) when I face troublesome times: "But He said to me, My grace (My favor and loving-kindness and mercy) is enough for you [sufficient against any danger and enables you to bear the trouble manfully]; for My strength and power are made perfect (fulfilled and completed) and show themselves most effective in [your] weakness."

Again, our prayers are with you, keep the faith, pray without ceasing, give thanks in all things, count it all joy as you go through and offer up a sacrifice of praise, and know that like Job, God will give you double for your trouble. God bless you. We love you and you are not alone. In fact, pray with me right now, for where two come together as touching and agreeing on anything it shall be done.

"Father God, in the mighty and wonderful name of Jesus, we come before You knowing You have everything already worked out in this situation. Father, we pray You comfort all those who are victims of hurricane Katrina. We pray You give them peace and assurance that You have a plan and You are working it out as we speak. Father, heal those who are grieving the loss of loved ones. Heal those who are ill or hurt. Provide for all the needs of Your people. Father, we pray for quick restoration of homes, jobs, and businesses, but until then we pray each and every person be given a safe and loving place to reside and fellowship. Father, we pray that this event will not be a traumatic scar on the hearts and minds of Your people, but a chance for everyone to show brotherly love. Father, we pray You open up the hearts of people all over the world to give generously to provide for those in need, whatever the need, that no one will go lacking. We ultimately pray Your will be done. Amen and amen."

Now believe it and receive it.

Cynthia A. Williams
Newport News, VA

Although the storms blow and the waters rise. The Lord still sees you through the compassion in His eyes. It may not seem as though He cares. Yet in each sorrow, there is a part that He shares. Remember His words in your most dire straits. Renewed strength is promised for those who wait (Isaiah 40:31). This is your night for weeping to endure. Joy is coming in your morning, in that rest assured (Psalm 30:5). The nation and the world hold you up in prayers to the one true and living God, and yes...He still cares (1 Peter 5:7).

Pastor Samuel M. Wright, Jr.
Union, NJ

⌒ᐗᖬᐗ⌒

To you my brothers and sisters I would like you to know that my fervent prayers are with you. During this time when you may be experiencing countless thoughts and emotions please remember that God does love you. During this time when you may feel weak, confused, or distressed be strong because He is able to use you and show you that you may not be as weak, confused, and distressed as you think you are. You may be the very person the God uses to be the "rock" for someone who may not be as strong as you. They may be watching how you are handling your situation and that thing may be just enough to give them strength to carry on another day, week, month, or year.

Remember 2 Corinthians 4:8-9 which says "We are troubled on every side, yet not distressed; we are perplexed, but not in despair; persecuted, but not forsaken; cast down, but not destroyed." Also I want to encourage you with the words Jesus said in John 16:33 "These things I have spoken unto you, that in me ye might have peace. In the world ye shall have tribulation: but be of good cheer; I have overcome the world."

⌒ᐗᖬᐗ⌒

I love you as I love myself and I pray that you enjoy good health and that all may go well with you, even as your soul is getting along well, in the name of Jesus.

George Dorton III
Fayetteville, GA

⌒ᐗᖬᐗ⌒

And Jesus said unto them, "Come unto Me all you who labor and are heavy laden, and I will give you rest. Take my yoke upon you and learn of Me for I am meek and lowly in heart, and I will give rest unto your souls. For My yoke is easy, and My burden is light" (Matt. 11:28-30). Although He is a very compassionate Father, He does not want His children to wallow in self-pity or frustration. In times of difficulty, His desire is that we call upon Him and take advantage of His infinite capacity to deal with all situations. His word is an encouragement and an every-ready source of strength. Here He reminds us that when our problems are too heavy for us, He is waiting for His people to permit Him to handle them. In Psalms 50:15, He says "Call upon Me in the day of trouble. I will deliver you, and you shall glorify Me." In Psalm 34:7, we are told "The angel of the Lord encamps all around those who fear Him and delivers them." In Psalm 36:7, we are reminded "How precious is Your lovingkindness, O Lord, that the children of men put their trust under the shadow of Your wings." He has never yet failed to keep a single promise.

B.T. Prince, Jr.
Charlotte, NC

Aftermath

The gray clouds disperse.

Leaves sparkling like diamonds.

God's promise appears.

The Rock

The rock! The rock!

The forces of evil rage

Around me like a wildfire!

Fears, doubts, and failures

Howl fiercely within me,

But I will stand. I WILL STAND

On the Rock, on the Rock!

That Rock is Jesus!

Hard to believe that I wrote that first poem nearly thirty years ago, but I have experience now that proves it to be true, which is why I could write the other poem five years ago. No matter what hardship or darkness that you may pass through if you stand on the Rock when the storms end you will be standing and you will see God's hand in the storm and His promise in the sky. May He grant you great wisdom and peace through His Son, Jesus Christ!

Dr. Ronald Shultz
Terrell, TX

⁓ᘓ᷃ ᷄ᘐ⁓

My dearest friend, my heart is broken for you. Katrina's rampage evoked both tears of compassion and prayers for deliverance. My desire was to be there; to do something, but time and circumstances prevented me from coming. But there is Someone who is there. His name is Jesus Christ.

The Old Testament speaks of the coming of Jesus – "And he shall be as the light of the morning, when the sun riseth, even a morning without clouds…" (2 Sam. 23:4). Jesus was the hope of the future.

Friend, through all this darkness, a light shines! Through all this devastation, there is hope! There will be better days. Jesus is our Morning without Clouds! The Bible says "that whosoever calls upon the name of the Lord shall be saved." If you don't know Christ as your Savior, why not invite Him into your life today? To my brothers and sisters in the Lord, we love you; we pray for you; we stand with you in your struggles. Let our Loving Heavenly Father be your hope in building your future.

Skeet Keaton
Taunton, MA

I stand at your edge and feel the gentle ripple of your waves rolling in and out across the imprint of my feet. You caress the sand and return to the depth of your soul. The wind stirs and washes a cooling spray upon my sun-drenched face. I am renewed.

Parched and weary, I take in your sustenance. You replenish me and I am grateful. I drink and I am refreshed. I am immersed in you and I am cleansed.

Oh, raging sea and water, how can it be… that what lulls me to sleep on a summer's night betrays my heart and floods my home? What is this force within you that calls you to impale destruction on these shores? I stand upon the shore again and sense your sorrow. My tears mingle with the shower of your salty wake.

The scarlet-purple hue of sunset dips behind your distant edge and the promise of tomorrow blows soft upon the evening wind. The Spirit of my God breathes tender healing on my soul. I will return again to the mystery of your shores. I will remember His footprint on the sands of my life. I will remember...always...how He loves me.

Eleanor Marshall Manning
Troy, NY

Heaven's Light

Lightning bolt and moonbeam,
Falling star and rainbow;
Don't you know,
Heaven gives light in the darkness.

Northern lights and star dust,
Comet blaze and galaxy glow;
Don't you know,
Heaven gives light in the darkness.

In dark days and the storm,
In the night and heavy rain,
Hope eases away the pain –
As heaven gives light in the darkness.

Heaven provides light in deepest dark.
Look for it and catch the spark.
Don't give in to fear and dismay.
Light shines forth to show the way.
Heaven … sheds forth hope in the darkness.

Lightening bolt and moonbeam,
Falling star and rainbow;
Don't you know,
Heaven gives light in the darkness.

Northern lights and star dust,
Comet blaze and galaxy glow;
Don't you know,
Heaven gives light in the darkness.

Love and goodness cast a light,
In days of sorrow and of grief,
Warming hearts – hope brings relief,
As heaven gives light in the darkness.

Heaven provides light in deepest dark.
Look for it and catch the spark.
Don't give in to fear and dismay.
Light shines forth to show the way.
Heaven … sheds forth hope in the darkness.

Yes…heaven gives light, heaven gives light, surely, heaven
gives light in the darkness!

(Shine. Look up! Take hope!)

Key Scripture:
"Those who are wise will shine like the brightness of
the heavens, and those who lead many to righteousness
like the stars for ever and ever" (Daniel 12:2).

Personal Note:
In my darkest days God reminded me of His love through
those kind souls and loving signs that lit up my world and
brought hope and a star to follow. If I looked at these heav-

enly lights, instead of focusing on the darkness around me, then I truly was able to face another moment, another hour, another day and carry on in a world of chaos and sorrow. I had lost everything, my home, my honor, my children, my health... it all. I wrote these lyrics to express the deep lesson He taught me in the midst of my anguish. May it encourage you to look up and find those glimmers of light. God Be With You. The new life will come, one step at a time. I know, because through His help I have begun to rise from my ashes and so can you.

Alina Patterson
Tallahassee, FL

In the hour of trouble, nothing is as important as our faith in the unfailing love of God. Such faith is the spawning ground of hope and the pathway of effort. Most important, however, is the fact that faith gives voice to our desire to go on, to endure and to overcome every diversity. In faith we call on the Lord in our troubles, and He hears and He answers the cry of faith.

Reginald Lawrence
Randallstown, MD

The Bible declares that there is a time for everything. There is a time for mourning and a time for joy. I have realized that we do not question God during the times of joy, but we tend to do so during times of mourning. However if the truth be told, it is God who preserves us in both. It's His mercy that keeps us surviving and His grace gives us strength to stay alive. Hear me today, I have also been a victim of a hurricane, and I know that

God is able to keep your heart at peace even if your environment is in chaos. Allow Him to give you His peace; He has designed it for you. Today.

Jamall Petty
Nassau, Bahamas

⌒↶↶ ↶⌒

    I got out of school late one evening and it was almost dark. I had to walk home and it was almost two miles. A few blocks from my home the road narrowed down and passed through a thick overgrowth of trees, vines and bushes. I was afraid to pass this way in the dark. As I entered the woods, I suddenly heard a voice which said "Son, would you like for me to walk with you?" It was my father's voice. He took my hand and led me home. He couldn't take away the dark, but I felt safe with my hand in his.

    We live in a fast-changing world with many paths to choose from. Some of them lead through the darkness. We must learn not to choose our path, but simply let the Father lead us and then we will always be safe. Sometimes our paths lead through the bright sunlight. Sometimes our paths lead into the dark nights and we cannot always see, but the Fathers hand still leads. Sometimes there just doesn't seem to be a path to take, but the Father will make a way. We hear His comforting words "come follow me." In Him we find strength and hope. We must remember too that it takes the storms and rain before the sunlight can make a "Rainbow."

    When life is at its darkest hour, remember the sun will shine again. God bless all of you as we continue to remember you in our prayers.

Chester Veazey
Sperry, OK

⌒℮⸗ ⸗℮⌒

In Hebrews11:1, the apostle tells us that "Now faith is the substance of things hoped for, the evidence of things not seen." Often we are told that, in times of trial, we must have faith in Christ. To me, this means that the "substance of things I hope for" is in Christ. The evidence of things that God has in store for me, that I have neither seen nor imagined, are also in Christ.

When times get so tough that my heart is ready to fail me, I remember that in Christ is my hope and every blessing that God has in store for me. God does not create the bad things in our lives but He will use them to help us realize that our faith must be in Christ to survive what this world throws our way.

Pastor Bobby Keating
Bennettsville, SC

⌒℮⸗ ⸗℮⌒

For the survivors of Hurricane Katrina:

I want you to know first of all that you are blessed. Do you know why you are blessed? Because you are a survivor. The Lord said in His Word that "he will not leave you or forsake you" (Deut. 31:6). Be strong and of good courage, fear not, nor be afraid of them: for the LORD thy God, he it is that doth go with thee; he will not fail thee, nor forsake thee. 1 Chronicles 28:20: "And David said to Solomon his son, Be strong and of good courage, and do it: fear not, nor be dismayed: for the LORD God, even my God, will be with thee; he will not fail thee, nor forsake thee, until thou hast finished all the work for the service of the house of the LORD." So therefore, your service for the Lord right now is to work together, love one another and not fight against each other.

Pull together and build back New Orleans (to the great city

it used to be) or else you might bring judgment on yourselves again. So pray this prayer with me: Father God, I am thankful that you spared my life and gave me a second chance. I ask that you forgive my sins. I know it was you, because I could not help myself. I know it was the enemy that tried to destroy me, because you said so in your Word, in John 10:10, "The thief cometh not, but for to steal, and to kill, and to destroy: I am come that they might have life, and that they might have it more abundantly. So, this is my prayer to you, that it is God's will that you live and live a prosperous life. So work together, build together, love one another, help one another in times like these. May the Lord bless you and keep you, make his face to shine upon you and give you peace. Amen.

Pastor McKinley Williams
Bethany Non-Denominational Ministries
Bridgeport, MI

⁀ᴄ₊ ₊ᴐ⁀

This past Sunday our church put away the sermon and got down on our knees and faces for you. We talked about your pain and trauma and how much devastation there has been for you to endure. We cried for you. We asked God to watch over you and your families. We asked the Lord to supply everything you need to get through this. We prayed for God to show us what we could do for you.

A man stood up in the service and said there were refugees coming into our area and homes were needed for them when they arrived. When my husband and I came home, he called about that and we were put on a list to take a family in. We want to do everything we can.

A few days ago, I received an email from a man in London who wanted to send a donation to our ministry so he could help. I told him that he could send his gift through Western

Union and I didn't hear from him until this morning. When I opened his e-mail, he had written that he and his wife were sending $50,000 to our ministry so we could help with the victims of hurricane Katrina. We are praying as I write this, asking God to show us where He wants us to help. I have never seen such generosity as this.

My friends, I'm seeing a great thing happen. In the midst of this terrible tragedy, God is causing a great love to rise up all around the world for all of you. I don't know you, but I love you and I want to dry your tears and make the days better for you. I want to help give you your life back with an abundance added to it.

In the Bible when Job lost everything, including his children, his health, his livestock, and way to make a living, he saw how the Lord will step in and restore a life. The Lord gave him back more than he originally had and the enemy was never allowed to touch Job again. I pray this for you, too. You and I may never meet, but I offer this prayer to you today. May God bless you every day for the rest of your life.

Lord, my friends are hurting. Lord, my friends need You. We have never had to deal with a situation like this before so we don't know what is to come still or how to make it all turn around. But Lord, we know You and You are the giver of life. You are the Restorer of life. In fact, You say You are Life. We lean hard into You right now for their sake. They are in need of many things and You know each and every person and what they're going through.

You know the challenges and the setbacks. But You also know the future is full of hope for them. As they draw near to You, You will draw near to them and they will see the blessings from that. You, Oh Lord, are their shelter and their mighty fortress.

I pray for every baby, every child, every parent, every elderly person. I pray that You, Lord, will pull them up and out of this misery and give them a new song to sing, full of joy and laughter. Help them to know there is life after the flood. Open Your Word to them and let them see Your promises are forever.

Amen

Pastor Laura Smith
Laingsburg, MI

⁓ᴄ₊ ₅ᴐ⁓

To all my sisters and brothers who suffered through the raging madness of Hurricane Katrina, please know that the world is with you, for we are all one spirit clothed in flesh.

I pray that your new life in the coming days will be better than you ever dreamed that it could be. I pray that your tears will turn to laughter, and that your pain and sorrow will turn into joy and peace. I pray that in your darkest moments you will see the bright ray of hope that shines in front of you and that your faith be strengthened by it. Faith is the evidence of things not seen, but the hope for them and without faith, there is no hope, for faith is like a moonless night that brings forth darkness as a promise of the light to come.

I pray that all of the wounds that Katrina left behind be healed and that you remember them naught. I pray that by the evidence of the love that is showered upon you that you know that God is alive and well for God and love are one just as we are all one.

One can always ask Lord, where were you when I was walking alone? And The Lord answered... My child, you did not walk alone. The set of footprints that you saw behind you were left by me when I carried you in my arms.

Judy Azar LeBlanc
Mesa, Arizona

⁓ ᒉ ᔫ ⁓

In Psalm 107 it states the following:

"Give thanks to the Lord for He is good; his loves endures forever....They were hungry and thirsty, and their lives ebbed away. Then they cried out to the Lord in their trouble, and He delivered them from their distress...They were glad when it grew calm, and He guided them to their desired haven" (vv. 1,5,30, NIV).

When trouble and hard times hit, God is closer to us then we even imagine. All we have to do is call on Him and believe. No matter what yesterday was like or what has happened in your past, God is waiting for you and ready to give you a new tomorrow. I believe God saved you from the destruction for a reason—I'm believing that God is going to turn your situation, attitude, and outlook on life totally around. I'm believing your best days are ahead and you have not peeked in life as of yet. The storm blew and gave you it's best shot—but look, you are still standing—you have not been wiped out. Yes, your earthly "things" have been taken away-but not you! If you can make it thru this, you can make it thru anything!

Lord, I pray for my brothers and sisters reading this right now, Lord, I pray you will complete the perfect plan you have for each one of them. I pray that if they have not been serving you with all of their heart, mind and soul-they will totally surrender their lives over to you right now. Give them the peace, direction, and joy they have been desiring. And Lord I pray that they will be a witness to others that are or will be going thru something traumatic and they will give comfort to those who need comfort, as they have been comforted in their time of need. Thank You, Lord, for giving each one of them boldness to step out to be a mighty witness in these days ahead and giving them the words when they need them the most. Thank You, Lord, for turning their situation around and for answering our prayers. In Jesus' name, amen.

God Bless,

Rev. Brent Bozarth
Pasadena, CA

⌒℃ₑ ₅⌒⌒

Having lived through several hurricanes in North Carolina, I have witnessed first hand what a hurricane is capable of doing. I have viewed many images of the devastation that a hurricane can bring on a community, but I can't begin to comprehend the level of devastation left in Katrina's path, but thankfully, God can and does. God is always with you, in good times and bad. A hurricane can destroy everything in its path, but God's love for you can NEVER be destroyed. God is with you, and when you trust in God, you're never alone.

Brandon Lee Boswell
Jacksonville, NC

⌒℃ₑ ₅⌒⌒

We live in an insecure world. Disasters that are out of our control strike us. Psalm 12:12 informs us we can look to God from whom our strength comes. He made the heavens, the earth and mountains, and yes, the water. This is His world and He knows it and all that is upon it intimately. The psalm states this Creator God, who knows us intimately will not let us out of his sight. God never sleeps, or even slumbers. The Bible says, Your Guardian God won't fall asleep. Not on your life! Israel's

Guardian will never doze or sleep" (The Message).

God is our guardian right by our side all of the time to protect us from every evil. He guards you now, and He guards you always. We may face unpleasant circumstances, but we can rest with certainty knowing God is right by our side wherever we may be. In every situation of life, God provides calmness, comfort, companionship and security for each of us. When we doubt His presence, we only need to ask Him to show Himself to us by giving us assurance and peace. Let us be strong in the Lord and the power of His might.

Carolyn Jean Duecker
Richmond, IN

If we live long enough on this earth we will go through trials and witness the trials of others. I have found that if we search for the rainbows even during this overwhelming situation Jesus quiets our hearts. He reveals His presence in our midst and gives us a peaceful assurance that we are in His hands. The Psalmist David says it so clearly as though he wrote this on a clear day filled with rainbows, "The Lord is my light and my salvation, whom shall I fear?" (Psalm 27:1).

Today, if we look around, we can see the rainbows of His presence and His presents in His faithfulness of His indelible, unfailing Word. His rainbow lights are revealed in the shared lives of His people who reflect His love into the rooms of our hearts. We are never homeless with Jesus. He opens our eyes to see the rays of light flowing from the porthole of heaven. He dispels the darkness with His very presence because He is light (1 John 1:4-5) and the light of His glory fills your heart as you look to Him for rainbows. We praise Him as the psalmist,

"Praise Him, sun and moon, praise Him, all you shining stars!" (Psalm 148:3).

Julie Chauvin
Katy, TX

The cycle of life ordained by God was seen on that awful day.
A baby was born and an old man died and many were
   wracked with pain.
But in the midst of the flood and rain and in the midst of
   your horror,
There is a God that gives life again that leads you into safe
   harbor.
Life is not the material things that we search so hard to find,
But in the love of a Savior's eyes who looks with love on
   mankind.
The strength we need is found in his arms and in the warmth
   of His presence.
These are the things that a life is made of so let us stop and
   give reverence,
To the one who made us just as we are and sees each tear as it
   falls.
He is the Lord of the earth, sea and sky—He is the Lord
   of us all.
Take heart my dear friend in the days ahead and know that
   we care and we love you.
We are your friend and God is your God, you and I are
   brothers so
Don't let them tell you ever again that we are not linked to
   each other.
May God give you peace as you face each day with new
   determination and give you the path that leads you
   home, wherever it is in our nation.

God bless you and keep you is my fervent prayer!

Dorothy Lyons
Indian Shores, FL

⌐ ⌐ ⌐ ⌐

To those who have lost loved ones, homes and perhaps even hope for the moment because of Hurricane Katrina let me say, God has not forgotten you. It is easy to say some good will come out of this but even harder to actually live out the promise of Romans 8:28, which says, "And we know that all things work together for good to those who love God...." Let me remind you that life is short and you must go on and continue to trust Him, and you know full well He will never leave or forsake you. Just in case you think this is an idle encouragement from someone high and dry and unaffected by a deadly hurricane I will tell you this. I lived less than a mile from where the hurricane broke through the industrial canal levee and my house, car and my church are completely underwater even as I write these words. I am not rich and my insurance barely covers the cost of my house. So I speak as one among the victims of this great ordeal. I can only tell you what I hear the Holy Spirit telling me, God loves you and will help you to recover. And if it helps at all I love you too, all of you from Louisiana, Mississippi, and Alabama. You are my neighbors and fellow sufferers and God is our helper. One thing I should point out is that I have written a book entitled *An American Prophet and His Message* published by the same publisher as the book you are reading. I commend them for their interest in publishing this book of encouragement and I'm glad I chose them to be my publisher.

Dear friends don't lose hope because thousands, perhaps millions of believers around the globe are praying for us. Add to that the knowledge that we have the God who created all there is to support us. We will overcome.

In Christ's love,

Rev. Michael Bresciani
Arabi, LA
http://americanprophet.org

Rainbow After the Storm

Sometime it takes a little time for the Rainbow to show up after the storm, but when conditions are right it can be seen coming from many different directions. That's the way God's Rainbow of love and compassion comes through His creation to those that have experienced great loss through the storms of life. God's Rainbow of love and help can be seen coming in many different colors from many different directions. You can be sure this Rainbow will always appear, and with it comes the promise of a new day to all that look for it. May God's mighty hand lead and protect you in the days ahead. Your Friend, Love

T J Collins
Greenwood, SC

Thank You for the Brokenness

Thank You Lord for my insecurity that I would seek Your strength as my scaffolding.

For the storms of life that have deprived me of everything I had, that I might truly appreciate my riches in You.

For the stalking melancholy that violates me at will and makes my confused thoughts cry after for Your wisdom.

For the arrows of guilt that waste my flesh, so that I might find refuge behind the outspread arms of Your Cross!

For the black boot of shame pressing my head into the mud, so that Your voice of love might become so tender, crying a thousand "Hosannas," into my whimpering breast.

For the fears of failure, the gnats that consume hope, that Your "rod and staff" might revive my heart.

For the many rejections that have doubled me over, that Your Words, "I will never leave nor forsake you," make me dance.

For my weaknesses that I dare not even whisper, that You might be my strength and confidence.

For the poverty I can not escape (though I tried with all my strength), that You might become my treasure and my life.

The better I see myself, the more beautiful You are.

Daniel Mann
Brooklyn, NY

God Is Very Present

"God is our refuge and strength, a very present help in trouble. Therefore will not we fear, though the earth be removed, and though the mountains be carried into the midst of the sea; Though the waters thereof roar and be troubled, though the mountains shake with the swelling thereof."—Psalm 46:1-3 (KJV)

When all is well we tend to feel close to God; the greater our pain the more distant He seems. Perhaps nothing could be farther from the truth, however. God is always present, but in times of trouble He is very present. That's why in life hope keeps triumphing over despair, testimonies over tests, and rebirth over devastation. Happy are we who trust God as our refuge, our strength, and our help in times of trouble. Doing so does not exempt us from the storms of life; rather it gives us peace in the midst of them.

Dear Lord, thank You for being closest to me when You seem farthest away. Amen.

Frank King
Savannah, GA

Beyond What I Can See

Time and time again the Bible tells us many stories of people whose faith, when put into action made the difference in their life. Some were healed of sickness and disease; others gave their last two pennies. People pushed their way through crowds just to touch the hem of His clothes, they climbed trees to get a better look at Him and they traveled great distances just to hear Him speak the words of healing for their loved ones. Whatever their act of faith, they all believed that Jesus would do for them what He had done for others. They had faith beyond their circumstances, beyond what they could see for the moment.

Too many times we get bogged down in living for the moment. Our faith goes only as far as we can see down that road. Peter had the same issue when he jumped out of the boat to walk on the water to where Jesus was, and as soon as the waves blocked his view of Jesus he began to sink. If the road is not clear, many of us question our faith or God's faithfulness to us and like Peter we begin to sink. There are times when we just can't see where God is leading, but like so many others before us we must rest assured in whom we have believed and carry on, even beyond what we can see.

So many times I have failed God, and in my weak faith I began to sink. The trials of this life have circled their wagons and camped out around our door step many times. Through it all my wife and I have learned to trust in God, even when the road has not been clear and indecision is everywhere. Through it all we have learned that God is faithful. Not one single promise has He left unfulfilled, according to His will for us. I am forever thankful that His love and grace exceeds beyond what I can see, beyond my circumstances and beyond my faith. In those times that I have broken His commands, He still sets me free, because His love for me exceeds beyond what I can see. When all I can see is a life of selfish ambition filled with self serving decisions, then God lets me know that He sees beyond what I can see; that He has a plan. He can take the mess I have made and use it for His purpose; He turns around the mistakes of my life as He holds me in His arms, because He sees beyond what I can see.

Grace and Peace be with you.

Steve Kennard
Spring, TX

The Silence After the Storm

In the silence of His answer he calls to my soul, "Come closer and abide with me."
I seek and ask, yet am met with silence.
My tears flow with the pain of my heart, I come to Him, in His Presence where He resides:
The spirit realm of eternity.
He waits so I will not be lost when I arrive.
I seek.
I call.
I ask...
I walk the path of Truth so straight,
So clearly lit by His brilliant light.

I must walk to arrive.
I must do all that I can to reach out
And grasp His outstretched hand.
Though the gift I am given is free,
The taking of the gift is entirely up to me.

Aviella Shomayr
Mesa, AZ

God's Rainbow of Promises

The title of this book just about says it all. Sometimes when people have catastrophes come into their lives, they really need to reflect on the rainbow God sends to us in the storms of life. A rainbow is a beautiful ark that God arches across the sky. It is always seen in and through the storms. Actually, God's rainbow is only seen in the time of storms. When the storms are the darkest and the most ferocious, the rainbow shines the brightest. God's blessed rainbow can be seen through the darkest storms.

God's rainbow always represents His promises to us. The great promises of God shine the brightest when we need them the most. The rainbow referenced in Genesis 9: 13- 14 conveyed God's promises to His people. When we look out into the storms and see God's magnificent rainbow, we know all is well. God is still in charge and His great promises hold true.

As you know, an ark is sometimes defined as a conveyance that takes something from one place to another. Noah's ark conveyed him and his family through the great flood and saved their lives. Only eight people of earth were saved as the ark transported them through the waters to dry land. Then, God sent His rainbow at that time to convey His promises to the people. The ark of the rainbow is just one of the beautiful arks God sends our way in times of great need.

To save Moses' life when he was an infant, God helped his mother fashion an ark that would transport her young son from sure death as a Hebrew slave to life in the palace of the Egyptian King. This ark conveyed young Moses from being the son of a slave to being the son of a king.

Another ark provided conveyance for the Ten Commandments and God's mercy from the wilderness of Sinai to the people of God as they journeyed to the Promised Land. This ark represented God's presence with His people. This beautiful ark known as the Ark of the Old Covenant provided God's blessings and promises to the people during their most difficult times.

But, God has provided a much greater Ark for His people today. This Ark is Jesus Christ. It is this Ark who provides our transportation from death in this life to the wonderful glories of Heaven. Like the other arks mentioned, this Ark provides God's promises for the future to all of us. He comforts us; He consoles us in the here-and-now and He will always be available to us. We'll never have to go it alone. Jesus comes to us in the greatest storms of our lives and says, "Let not your heart be troubled, if you believe in God, believe also in me," (John 14: 1).

Jesus is the Ark of the New Covenant. Through Him, we find the hope, the fortitude, and the perseverance we need to face the storms of life. Jesus is the Ark who conveys us from the slavery of sin to be the Children of the King. God's ark of the rainbow is the conveyance that brings God's promises of care and divine providence down to earth. Trust Him!

Bill French
Saint Petersburg, FL

God Is Still In Control

Though the winds may blow and the rain may fall, Jesus is there to help you get through it all.

And just when it seems like all hope is gone, Jesus will guide your steps to help you continue on.

Keep your eyes focused on Christ, who is the Protector of your soul, And remember that God is still in control.

Samantha P. Meade
Petersburg, VA

Walk On In God

As water floods the earth, O God,
May your peace and love flood our souls.
You alone can cause calm in the chaos.
You alone can bring hope in hopelessness.
You turn our disaster to dreams
That again we may walk on, O God,
Into your purpose for our lives.
Help us to trust you in our distress
For then we will rise in success.
To You we give our hopes and our dreams
That we may bring glory to you, O God.

Dr. Kathy A. Bliese Walk
Grand Island, NE

Sailing Through Bloody Seas

Her home had just burned. The woman has lost most of her possessions. Yet she faced the camera and spoke confidently: "I'm thankful to God. I still have my family, my life and my faith. All that (pointing at the remains) is just stuff."

That "stuff" had been the valuable accumulation of a lifetime of possessions. Yet she was not defeated. She expressed a powerful, vibrant faith - a faith that is not common and never easy.

When I was a kid, our church used to sing a song with a verse that read: "Must I be carried to the skies on flowery beds of ease, while others fought to win the prize and sailed through bloody seas?" Indeed! It is not easy to sail through "bloody seas." Many in our affluent nation seem to view faith as simply a means to prosperity and success. That is part of the story of course; but there is much more.

Faith includes the power to carry us to victory through really bad things. And bad things do happen to good people. Biblical writers struggled honestly with this reality. Sometimes, like us, they got angry with God. The prophet Habakkuk was angry with God because of the injustice and violence he saw all around him. Why didn't God do something about it? After intense struggle, he concluded with a great song of victory:

> "Though the fig tree should not blossom,
>   nor fruit be on the vines,
> the produce of the olive fail
>   and the fields yield no food,
>   the flock be cut off from the fold
>   and there be no herd in the stalls,
> Yet will I rejoice in the Lord;
>   I will take joy in the God of my salvation."
>   (Habakkuk 3:17 - ESV)

Sailing through bloody seas is never easy. Yet it can become the basis of a living, dynamic and victorious faith.

Charles Turner
Greenville, TX

A Cry For Help

In the name of Jesus,
we ask You Lord-
to please help us
for we are weary and in need.

Give us courage.
Give us strength.
Give us wings to fly.
Let your will be done in us.

Teach us Lord to Love more in You,
-Hope more in You,
-Trust more in You.

Teach us to Fly higher
and to Shine brighter.

Teach us to pray more
in the quiet of our hearts.
- to Sing for all to hear,
- to Sing your praises
even in the darkness.

Let Your light guide us.
Let Your light guard us from evil.
Let Your light shine in us all.

Virgin Mary - intercede for us.
Angels - whisper to us.
Saints - pray for us.
Holy Spirit - help us
to hear You and see You in all,
give us discernment and wisdom.

Please, Jesus- Save us. Forgive us. Help us.
Pour your healing blood on us all and heal us.
Please, give us an understanding heart.

Thank you for providing all that we need.
Thank you for picking us up and carrying us.
Thank you for healing our broken heart
and making it whole once again.
Thank you for Your Love, Mercy, and Understanding.
Thank you for Your will in us all.

May everything be according to your will, Jesus.
May we act only in You, for you.

Thank you, Thank you, Thank you.
Thank you for giving us the strength
to Fly, Shine, and Sing.

Praise be Jesus, Our Lord.
Praise be, Praise be, Blessed be
the name of Jesus.

Aleluya, Aleluya, Aleluya. Amen

Isabel Maria Amaya
Atlanta, GA

Sure

She stood there perplexed. In the middle of all that was
happening, she dared to ask, "GOD WHERE ARE YOU?"
Her question was met with emotions of hurt, anger, confusion
and a lot of demand. She took a deep breath; trying to make a
decision that will without any doubt, change the course of her

life. As she wiped her tears, she said in her head, "Lord, I need help! Haven't I been faithful? Haven't I sacrificed and been obedient? Haven't I, haven't I, haven't I, the song sung," but in the mist of her concentrating on the point she was trying to make, she missed something that caused her to stop abruptly. "I didn't hear . . ." the tone was softer and one of question directed inside. She heard the Lord say something but in the middle of her listening to her, she missed it. That only sparked more tears as she moved in a direction that was unsure.

Unsure. It doesn't have an address but, it is definitely a location and sometimes, in the mist of the unsure, we miss it. Yet, God is faithful, He doesn't know any other way. I'm still learning that in the, "where are you" questions, God is asking the same. 'Where are you?'

Even in the unsure locations, He said that He would never leave you nor forsake you. He said He knows the thoughts that He thinks towards you, thoughts of peace and not of evil, to give you a future and a hope, even during the unsure, lack of understanding, hurt, confusion, where's and the why's, believe in Me. Trust Me.

Days later, as she thought back on the whole matter, it wasn't what she desired and yes, there were some losses along the way, but instead of looking at the losses, she looked at what she gained. She realized that in every situation it's an opportunity to reach another level in Him and if God decided to ask her, "Where are you?" her answer would be, a higher level of trust, another level of understanding and on my way to a location called Sure.

It is my deepest prayer that you will continue to trust in Jesus who is faithful and as you start over, remember, though your beginning 'again maybe' small, yet your latter will should greatly increasing.
(Jer. 29:11, Heb 13:5 and Job 8:6-7 KJV)

Tianna Che're Trezevant
Charlotte, NC

It Hurts

It hurts, it's so unbelievable, and it's a nightmare. But you are not alone. God still is. If only things could have been different, but you are not alone. God still is. God told Moses, "I AM THAT I AM." His very name comes from the root meaning "to be." Emmanuel means God with us. He became flesh and dwelt among us, and He promised that He is with us always. You will survive, as you are already a survivor. Through all of this, there is a bright side. You have survived! You have survived in order to live. It may appear presently that you are just existing, but His name is life and He loves you so very much. He loves you so much, and He has placed those around you to demonstrate that love. God has cried with you.

When Jesus beckoned Peter to Him out on the water, Peter got out the boat and walked on water as long as he kept his eyes fixed on Jesus. When he lost focus, he began to sink. We are out of the boat, and we can't lose our focus, and that is Jesus. He is still God, and His name Emmanuel assures us that God is with us.

We bless you in this time that you are given relief in Jesus' will. We bless your families, your hurt, your pain, and your life. We pray that you will know the saving grace of Jesus without a shadow of a doubt, that you will live to continue this gospel story as your part in this story unfolds. We pray that you will hear God more clearly; that you will see Him work in marvelous ways and then that you will share it through loving one another. It hurts now, but it will get better. GOD STILL IS GOD!

Rev. Dr. Emily Annette Pardue
Detroit, MI

Words of Encouragement
God is With Us

In life we face many storms;
They may come spiritual or natural.
Yet, God is with us through them all.

God will never let us fall, God will keep us
And let us stand tall. In spite of our need,
Pain or lost, God is here to relieve us.

God shines His wonderful and supernatural
Love on us. God lets His love shine through His
People and His overflowing Grace brings rays of
Sunshine for a better tomorrow. Our heavenly father,
God makes all things new; and Father we still trust You.

God you are a restorer of dreams, visions, health, families,
Wealth, lives and most of all a restorer of love.
In spite of hurricanes and storms, God, You let us
Laugh again, cry again, rebuild again, dream again,
Have good health again, have wealth again, live again, pray
    again
Believe again, see our families again, have Faith again and
    love again.

Shirley Ann Baldwin
Dearing, GA

I Have Much To Offer!

I heard your cries, and I saw your tears, I felt your anger, and
knew all your fears; I saw the water rising and knew what
would be, Because nothing can be hidden from ME.

For you, I have a reason, and hold a mighty plan, But if you do not believe, you will not understand; I know what I must do to meet your every need, But until WE come together, MY plan cannot succeed.

You may have lost everything and all that is left is ME! But I can give you eternal love if you love ME recklessly. I offer comfort, peace, strength, hope, as you have heard, And when you feel hunger, you can feed on MY Word!

You can become a worthy servant if you choose to serve ME, I know when you read MY WORDS, you wonder how could life be? MY child, I promise to care for you and I shall never cast you away, Your life shall become brighter when you start trusting ME today!

I promise everyone who sacrifices life for ME, will always live on, Receiving a hundred times over in riches, MINE are never alone; You may suffer persecution as I, too, suffered and chose to do, But your sins will be forgiven when confession comes from you!

"I pray not for the world, but for them who are MINE."

Love,
GOD

Jeanie Cline
Lenoir, NC

Through the Storm

The eyes of your children far away
they shed so many tears
it is for them I pray

My heartfelt prayer is they would see
that God loves them and will set them free

I wonder if they know you Lord,
I pray they do,
they need you so.

The death and destruction
beyond my grasp
what can I do to bridge the gap
What one thing could I provide
a prayer, some aid, time from my life?

I pray God's people would unite,
we have the power to save their lives
to show them love, compassion, faith
the time is now, no time to waste.

Although sorrow fills them in every way
let them know that if they pray,
that one day, not so very far away
the Lord will show them a brand new day.

Heidi Frederick
Campbell, CA

Bitter Waters Sweet
(Exodus 15:22-26)

The children in the wilderness, the Red Sea swallowed up
    their foe
The power of the Lord their God, unto them He did show

Moses led them on their journey, to God they sang their
    praise
Their music turned to murmur, and in only three short days

When in this land so barren, no water could be found
But for the pools of Marah, where bitter waters did abound

Moses cried unto the Lord, and He showed to him a tree
Into the waters it was cast, the waters sweet as it could be

Our music turns to murmur, storm's tempests they abound
Pools of panic, doubt and fear, bitter waters all around

When we cry unto the Lord our God, he'll show to us a tree
On that cross He bore our sins, from pools of pain we'll be
    set free

Vicky Boatright
Bastrop, LA

Conquerors

Though all around you the world did fall
Yet here you are standing tall

Battered and torn by the storm
With no shelter to keep you warm

Out of the rubble you came
Knowing life will never be the same

By God's grace you were kept alive
And by His power you will survive

...We are more than conquerors through Him that loved us.
Romans 8:35-37

Dr. Eric Cooper
Mitchellville, MD

A Love Letter From Jesus to His Friends (John 15:14 "You are My friends if you do what I command.")

Come unto Me all you who are weary,
I promise to give you My rest.
Take My yoke upon you and learn about Me; Together we'll
weather this test.

For I am most gentle and humble in heart, And I am there
with you, My friend.
Yes, My yoke is easy and My burden light, My love and My
care never end.

I know what it's like not to live in a home, There was "no
room for Me in the Inn."
But I only wanted some room in their heart, For I came here
to die for their sin.

I know what it's like to feel lonely and sad, Betrayed and
    deserted, denied.
My friends fled in fear when I needed them near.
They said that they loved Me, but lied.

I too have known fear—tasted death on My breath, Like you
    folks overwhelmed by that flood.
When I chose not to flee My own death on that tree, My
    sweat was like "great drops of blood."

Well, I have returned to my Father in heaven, Reigning with
    Him by My side, And we are preparing a home just for
    you, A mansion that's fit for a bride.

While you're still on earth, your heart is My home, I'll be
    with you always, you'll see.
But you can't imagine what glory awaits you When you come
    to live here with Me.

Annette Adams
Concord, TN

Why Lord?

In times of trial, we all ask, "Why Lord?"

But, many things are beyond our human understanding.

Our choice:
- be angry at God for allowing tragedy
- let God get us through the trial and see what He has to
  teach us

Without trial, we don't grow.

And after all else is gone, God is still there.

His eye is on the sparrow, and I know He watches me.

It is His eternal Kingdom we seek, not earthly things..

Through every hand and heart that touches you, you see Jesus face to face.

" And you will be secure, because there is hope." Job 11:18

Danny Moore
DeSoto, TX

Don't Waste Your Sorrows

"You keep track of all my sorrows. You have collected all my tears in your bottle. You have recorded each one in your book" (Psalms 56:8 NLB).

Few, if any, escape the heartaches and trials of life—life's sorrows! In fact, Job, who certainly knew the meaning of sorrow, said: "But mankind is born for trouble as surely as sparks fly upward" (Job 5:7 - HCSB). While such a thought seems to be excessively cynical, a second look at that thought will often prove to be true in one's life.

Our text offers a promise with which one might view his sorrows, that, while not necessarily removing them, offers Godly solace and comfort. "You keep track of all my sorrows. You have collected all my tears in your bottle. You have recorded each one in your book" (Psalms 56:8 NLB). Most of us would like to have someone who will listen as we rehearse our sorrows but usually find the old axiom to be true: "Laugh and the world laughs with you; cry and you cry alone" -

Horace (65-8 BC). What peace there is when we realize that not only is the Father aware of our heartaches but collects the tears we shed and recorded them in His book!

The old Hymn by Frank E. Graeff powerfully describes God's care for us in times of sorrow:

Does Jesus care when my heart is pained
Too deeply for mirth or song,
As the burdens press, and the cares distress And the way grows weary and long?

Refrain
Oh yes, He cares, I know He cares,
His heart is touched with my grief;
When the days are weary, the long nights dreary, I know my Savior cares.

Does Jesus care when my way is dark
With a nameless dread and fear?
As the daylight fades into deep night shades, Does He care enough to be near?

Does Jesus care when I've tried and failed To resist some temptation strong; When for my deep grief there is no relief, Though my tears flow all the night long?

Does Jesus care when I've said "goodbye"
To the dearest on earth to me,
And my sad heart aches till it nearly breaks, Is it aught to Him? Does He see?

James gave wonderful encouragement and instruction when he said: "Consider it a great joy, my brothers, whenever you experience various trials, knowing that the testing of your faith produces endurance. But endurance must do its complete work, so that you may be mature and complete, lacking nothing. Blessed is a man who endures trials, because when he passes the test he will receive the crown of life that He has promised to those who love Him" (James 1:3-4, 12 HCSB).

Peter taught the ultimate value of our sorrows by saying, "You rejoice in this, though now for a short time you have had to be distressed by various trials so that the genuineness of your faith— more valuable than gold, which perishes though refined by fire—may result in praise, glory, and honor at the revelation of Jesus Christ. You love Him, though you have not seen Him" (1 Peter 1:6-8 Holman HCSB).

So, dear friend, there is merit and significance to your sorrows, so don't waste them. Instead of languishing in your sorrows, look up! Let them lead you to a deeper and more profound relationship with the Lord. With Him no sorrow is wasted. He takes everything that comes on us on Himself and gives us His peace instead—the peace that passes all understanding. Instead of being consumed with your sorrows, lift them up to Him and rejoice that He cares more than you can possibly imagine.

Jefferson H. Floyd
Noblesville, IN

❦

When your life spirals out of control and changes forever, remember that the God of heaven and earth is still in control. His name is Jesus Christ. A verse that God gave me to share with others after my life spiraled out of control and changed forever was this:

In Romans 15:13 "Now may the God of Hope fill you with all joy and peace in believing that you may abound in hope in the power of the Holy Spirit."

The 'Now' in that verse is today and every day that you exist on earth. God is able to fill you with His joy and peace regardless of your circumstances but you must believe Him. It is done in God's power not your own strength. But you need to ask Him to do this for you and He will.

Dear Lord,

Please fill all the hurricane victims and workers that are trying to help them with Your peace and joy as the God of Hope that only You are able to do for them. We know that your peace passes all understanding and Your hope and joy will carry them through this trying time that they are experiencing. May they also be able to look back one day and realize that You were with them through all this and that You did not abandon them in their circumstances. May they know Your love that is infinitely above anyone else's and embrace them where they are at so that they might know You personally for eternity.

In Christ name,

Barbara Acocello
Irmo, SC

༺ ༻

You have survived the worst, but not alone. You survived for a purpose, God's purpose. Draw closer to God and he will draw closer to you. May the love of God comfort your entire being, your family and friends – for God said,

"… I know the plans I have for you, declares the LORD, plans to prosper you and not to harm you, plans to give you hope and a future." [Jeremiah 29:11 NIV] You can do all things through Christ, which is your strength. There is surely a future hope for you, and your hope will not be cut off.

Padrika Gray
Jacksonville, FL

༜ C ⸱ ༉ ༜

The Bible says that Jesus Christ is the firstborn of all creation and that by Him all things were created (Col. 1:15-16). It is a great comfort to know that God gave us Jesus Christ for the joy of our salvation. He healed the sick, raised the dead, and fed thousands on numerous occasions. Isn't it a great comfort to know that He is still taking care of us even today through His great works? Thank God we have people who really care about others and are willing to help in the most difficult of times. Thank God for the missionaries, nurses, doctors, military, and volunteers who lovingly sacrifice their time, money, and talents to help others. Just imagine most are total strangers, but because of the mercies from God put in their hearts, they lovingly help even when it is a dangerous situation. Thank you God for sending us such a loving example through Jesus Christ. May He always bless the lives of those in greatest need, and may they stretch their arms out to you for your help. You are our help in times of trouble; there is none greater. Oh have mercy on your people! Bring us from the valley of despair that we may serve you and recognize that you are our God. Thank you God for loving us all, we want to be your living image. Thank you Father!

Pastor Terry Eggleston
Laurel, MD

༜ C ⸱ ༉ ༜

Psalm 30:5 KJV tells us: "For his anger endureth but a moment;

in his favour is life: weeping may endure for a night, but joy cometh in the mourning." I can not fathom the ordeal that you are going through. I have been in the depths of despair myself. Wondering what to do next and what the future holds. I found that none really knows what the future holds but I know who is holding my hand, His love and Grace will be your Salvation and give you a peace that surpasses all understanding. Jesus Christ holds my hand and He will hold your hand too. All you have to do is just ask Him and He will. He will save you, love you, and help you through this ordeal. Our prayers and support are with you. You are our neighbors and we are supposed to treat you as we want to be treated. We will help you until you are on your feet and at home. God bless you and we salute your bravery and faith. Do not look back; look up your redemption draweth nigh.

Mark L. Washburn
Whitesboro, TX

We have a wonderful Lord who willingly died on the cross to pay the price for our sins. Trust Jesus Christ. Believe He did this for you and receive eternal life. When there are no cattle in the stalls - yet I will rejoice in the Lord, I will joy in the God of my salvation. Habakkuk 3:17-18

Livingston Blauvelt
Tallahassee, FL

Psalm 27:13 "I had fainted, unless I had believed to see the goodness of the LORD in the land of the living." King David, the writer of this Scripture, was obviously going through a trial, but he was confident that in this present life, God would see him through it!!! "I just as well give up the ghost, unless I trust God to see me through in this life and the after life." David is speaking to himself (and the reader) to stiffen his resolve!!! A person of faith must have teeth even when he or she is toothless!!!

Psalm 27:14 "Wait on the LORD: be of good courage, and he shall strengthen thine heart: wait, I say, on the LORD." There is a lot of heart trouble today among believers!!! It is known as faintheartedness, or the coward's heart!!! All of us have a little touch of it. How can this be cured? 'Wait on the Lord; be of good courage!!!.' When we are as low as we can go, look up.

God's got a blessing that Satan doesn't want us to see. Look up and anticipate the blessing. Look up and expect to receive it. Look up and thank God in the midst of the chaos. It will confuse the devil and show God the power of our praise. When we do that the Lord will strengthen our hearts. He is really the great...heart...specialist!!!

Rev. Will S. Kenlaw III
Silver Spring, MD

⌒℃ᷝ ᷤᴖ⌒

At the end of knowledge, turn to Jesus,
At the end of self, turn to Jesus,
He gave His Life,
So give Him your life,
At the end of everything, turn to Jesus.

Danny Moore
DeSoto, TX

⌒℃ᷝ ᷤᴖ⌒

Proverbs 3:5 "Trust in the LORD with all your heart, and lean not on your own understanding."

Hebrews 2:13 "I will put my trust in Him."

According to Webster, Trust is "assured reliance on the character, ability, strength, or truth of someone or something." Trust, through the eyes of the world is based on assured past performances that cause us to have trust in someone or something. It is hard for the world to put their trust in that which they cannot understand. This is in sharp contrast to the trust that God wants us to have in him and each other.

To lean not on our own understanding but put all our trust in God seems to go against our very nature. Yet the Bible is full of examples of men and women who reached down inside themselves and found the faith to trust against all odds. Matthew 14:28-29, Peter and the disciples are in a boat in the middle of the night, the seas were rough and the waves are rocking the boat. Suddenly they see the image of something coming towards them on the water and became very afraid. In the excitement of the moment Peter calls out "Lord, if it is You, command me to come to You on the water." For the moment, Peter had forgotten about the personal danger and called out to Jesus. Peter's act of faith was also an act of trust. Do you think Peter understood just how it was that Jesus was walking on the water? The disciples did not all huddle together in the boat to discuss what they were seeing or what they should do next. It was Peter, who in a moment of faith, called out to Jesus for him to come out on the water also. What's important about this story is Peter's faith to step out of the boat and trust in Christ. Notice none of the other disciples called out to Jesus. No one else jumped out of the boat but they could have. All the disciples could have gone to Jesus on the water and abandoned the boat but they did not. Peter was the only one who trusted enough in Jesus to commit himself to jump out of the boat

Recently the Lord brought back to my memory the words to a particular song "blessed are you when you trust but you just don't understand." These words really tell us the truth about what Peter did and what we need to do. When you don't understand why you can't find that job you need so badly, when you can't understand God's timing and things are looking bleak, when it seems you can't get any lower and you are down to your last ounce of faith and yet you still choose to trust. God honors faith that reaches up out of despair to trust that He will work things out. Anyone can trust in God when life is going well but when it's not, remember not to let your circumstances be like the waves that Peter saw and caused him to stop trusting. It was at that point when Peter took his eyes off Christ that he started to sink and it is the same with us.

Everyday we fight battles that can be like huge waves that threaten to overtake and consume us. The scriptures remind us that we shall overcome if we can just trust in God. Like Peter, call out to Jesus. He knows your circumstances and He cares for you. Trust in God, and again like Peter, He will lift you up in the middle of the storm.

Remember who you are in Christ, know that you are a joint heir to the Kingdom of God, trust in Him and keep holding on to your savior's hand.

Steve Kennard
Spring, TX

May the Lord God of Israel lift the tender and broken hearted in this, a time of trouble. May the Lord, the Father of our souls reach down and lift His people out of the mire, and

set them upon that Rock which will never be washed away.
Shalom to all who have passed through the waters!

Aviella Shomayr
Mesa, AZ

Faith is a journey.
For many days the many needs will call,
The many wants, the many wishes;
The dusks will seek the sleepless eyes to close, The dawns to open them, still filled with sleep,
For patience oft succumbs to crumbling walls That can no longer hold the longing in.
But strengthen now your patience and your faith, For your reward is near, the more to please
Since peace will be restored, no more to cease, As long as you remain within
The arms of God, the only source of peace.

Life is the journey that oft tests our faith.
God put us in a place to stand
And firmly trust, whatever may befall.
Though floods surround us with their roiling rage,
Like writhing snakes, like rumblings of decay,
Like arrows of accusing cries,
Like grabbing fingers, snapping snares,
Like tangles of arachnoid threads,
Like time imprisoned in a crowded space
And scratching, gnawing at the threshold
Of forced and aimless inactivity,
Demanding long longed-for release —
Still must faith prevail
And carry me until the land appears.....

And then we see the awesome sight:
It is a span of beckoning hue
Of melting colors, as they thaw
And then intensify their grandiose display,
Then stabilize and beckon still
With proclamations of their promises,
Tunneling unerringly beneath the bridge
Of fading colors, leaving yet
The silent promise written in the sky,
And gathering echoes now of whispers
Springing from the quietness,
Whispers of eternal voices
Speaking once again of peace:

I am the Alpha and Omega,
The beginning and the end.

                The promise of peace.

Elfriede Mollon
El Cajon, CA

Lord, my heart breaks and my tears flow along with the citizens who endure in the aftermath of Katrina's devastation. I know that you are the Healer, Lord, and you bring good through all situations to those who love you. Dear Holy One, I pray that you would open doors and prosper them in all areas of life; meet their needs for food, shelter, clothing, and a steady income; heal their hearts; ease their burdens; give them rest; bring them friends, both old and new; remind them that they have purpose; and inspire them to know the fullness of life that is found only in You. Amen.

"And we know that all things work together for good to them that love God, to them who are the called according to his purpose." Romans 8:28

Jennifer Loftin
Flint, MI

༄ ༄

Dear Hurting Friend,

As I prayed about words of comfort and encouragement, I asked those around me, "What would you say? What would you express to those who have lost so much?" And as I listened, I learned that many are not only giving of themselves, but are praying continually for you. But the words of my daughter, Mary, touched me deeply and I would like to share them with you.
   "Mom, tell them that Jesus cried too."

So now is the time to mourn. But in your tears, remember...
   The God of all creation
   The One who formed you
      in His image
      for a purpose
   Is ever-present and
      unchanging
   And He has a plan
      to comfort you.
   For our Lord experienced sorrow
      and unimaginable pain
   As He lay down His life
      that you may live.

Oh friend, He knows. Jesus knows
  hurt
  loneliness
  loss.
And because of this, He is
  ultimately
  uniquely
   qualified
  to offer hope.

"He heals the brokenhearted and binds up their wounds. Great is our Lord and mighty in power; his understanding has no limit." Psalm 147:3,5 (NIV)

Will you turn to Him today?

Leigh Ann Thomas
Sanford, NC

In the midst of despair
Know that God is still there.
He said that He would not leave
So to that promise cleave.
When it seems like all hope is gone
Rest in the fact that God is still on the throne.
For a reason don't search
Just know that He will not leave you in a lurch.
Let your faith work now more than ever before
Let love freely exude from your core.
Though what you have may not be plentiful
For the grace of God be thankful.
May God's blessings continue to sustain you in the midst of
  despair

Keep trusting because His presence is still there.
And of His miracles be aware
For He sees, knows and cares .

Marie Williams
Camden, SC

⌐ ⌐ ⌐ ⌐

Dear Traumatized Child of God,

You may feel like Job who lost everything dear to him; his livelihood, his servants, and his sons and daughters. As if that were not enough, he lost his health, and his friends accused him of sin. Yet he refused to renounce God. I encourage you to follow in Job's footsteps, looking to the Most High God for your help and sustenance. God was faithful to restore Job's fortunes and his family. He is no respecter of persons - - He can do the same for YOU, just believe. God is able to do superabundantly, far over and above all that we dare ask or think - - to HIM be glory! (See: Ephesians 3:20 AMP, Job 1, 2, 42)

Pastor Kathy Friend-Brumley
Broken Arrow, OK

⌐ ⌐ ⌐ ⌐

To All Who May Read This Passage:

And God said, "Behold, I am the Lord, the God of all flesh. Is there anything too hard for me?" (Jer 32:27 NKJV). The Lord is with us through every trial and test. He sees us through the storms of life, and the calamities that come to destroy us.

His Word says, that "we are hard pressed on every side, yet not crushed; we are perplexed, but not in despair; persecuted, but not forsaken; struck down, but not destroyed." (2 Cor. 4:8-9)

Life may be difficult right now, BUT NOTHING shall separate us from the love of God. "WE ARE CONQUERORS THROUGH HIM WHO LOVES US." (Rom. 8:37) IN OUR HEART, WE MUST TRUST AND BELIEVE!

Through the Lord's mercies we are not consumed, because his compassions fail not. They are new every morning; great is His faithfulness." (Lam. 3:22-23).

To all of the survivors of Hurricane Katrina, "GOD WILL PROVIDE!!" Stand Strong and Keep The Faith.

PEACE AND BLESSINGS!

Ms. Jina Lomax
Columbus, OH

⌒ᶜₑ ₅⌒

Our hearts throughout the country are weeping for the pain that you have experienced. The love that the Lord our God gives us will be passed onto you, so that you will be able to endure and get through this difficult time. Psalm 46:1 is a verse you should never forget. Take it with you always no matter where you go! "God is our refuge and strength, an ever-present help in trouble." The Lord will use his people to help you put the pieces of your life back together. Remember this: When you repent your sins to Jesus, he will grant you a blessing. When you ask him to live in your heart, he will fill your mind. When you thank him for being alive, he will make you happy. When you live for him, he will make you prosper! We truly have an awesome God!

Deborah Forrester
Parsippany, NJ

Hold on to my Hand.
… Look into my Face.
…I am here, and I am not going anywhere

I am here, now, holding onto you.
…and I will never let you go.

Do not listen to the storm…
… It's only noise.
Don't look at the waves…
… It's only water.

Hold onto my Hand,
…and Look into my Face,
… I am here, and I will never let you go.

What I give you is my Life…
Mine for yours… my blood for your sins,
I will never leave you. I will never forsake you, Now, and
always.

Michael A. Campbell
Clarksville, TN

"For God sent not his Son into the world to condemn the
world, but that the world through him might be saved." (John
3:17). In this you have the assurance that though your sins be
as a crimson stain, though your faults and failures be as
numerous as the fish in the sea, the blood of his Son Jesus has
been shed to cleanse you from all unrighteousness. Not so
much in the eyes of men, but in the eyes and soul of God.

May the hurricane be a turning point that you might realize that God, in his unfailing mercy and his infinite wisdom cares for you! And that he is concerned about you. And, that although you may be required to begin again from scratch, you can be of good cheer. "For we know that all things work together for good, for them that love God, to them who are the called according to his purpose. For whom he did fore-know, he also did predestinate to be conformed to the image of his Son, that he might be the first-born among many brethren." (Rom. 8:28-29)

Perhaps you may feel you are not called according to God's purpose. Perhaps you feel you are not as knowledgeable or spir-itual as some others may be. But rest assured. If you can believe on the name of God's Son Jesus, if you can believe that he came to earth to die in your place, you and we, have a record. "And this is the record, that God has given to us eternal life, and this life is in his Son (1 John 5:11). Everything about God, concerning you, is in His Son.

Geraldine Lewis
Las Vegas, NV

⌒ᶜᵉ ₔ⌒

"Come unto me, all ye that labour and are heavy laden, and I will give you rest." – MATTHEW 11:28

Father, I pray for all of the souls who have been adversely affected by Hurricane Katrina. I pray for Your mercy and compassion on each and every person who has experienced a loss. I pray for You to touch many lives with inspirational words written in this book. I pray that many will come to know that You are real, and when all else fails in life, You are always there.

Thank you, Father, for all You've done, and all You continue to do in our lives.

Jennifer M. Seibert
New York, NY

༺ ✿ ༻

God once told His people, in the Book of Isaiah, to "Fear not, for I have redeemed you; I have summoned you by name; you are mine. When you pass through the waters, I will be with you; and when you pass through the rivers, they will not sweep over you."

No one knows for certain why this disaster struck. But Christians are sure about some things: God exists, as does the sun when obscured by a cloud, even when we cannot see Him. God is still in control, even when it appears He is not. Life is brief. Circumstances can change overnight.

Sometimes God calms the storm, and other times, He calms His child in the midst of it. God knows you by name, and has spared you for a reason. The 3rd Act of your life has yet to be played out. This, too, shall pass. Nothing can touch you without first being allowed by God. Jesus was right there, suffering alongside you, as the wind and rain thrashed away outside, and as you went outside to see life, as you knew it, gone. God is the only permanent thing in this life. Good can come out of calamity, if we look for life lessons even in loss. We should never "waste" pain.

Your life was spared for a purpose. You can get through this crisis, if you take it just one day at a time.

What can we say to all of this destruction? Only that we must choose to become better, not bitter, from these experiences, for God can redeem the worst situations that come our way if we let Him. Once you are healed of the trauma you have endured, God can use you, as few others could ever be used, to pass along these precious promises to a person who is hurting just like you are now.

Even as you are reading these words, faithful Christians are giving to and serving in the relief work, and sending heavenward whispered prayers and good thoughts for you. So be certain that you are not alone. "Katrina" means to "purify". If we Americans will allow God do His redeeming work, bringing good even from things that appear to be evil such as hurricanes, then those ugly winds, and its dirty water, can awaken, cleanse, change, and grow us, and we will be the better for it. We will be able to look back on these dark days and smile, knowing that God caused enormous good to come from the very worst life could throw at us.

Oscar Reynold-Lynch
Queen Creek, AZ

When going through trials, tribulation and suffering, I encourage you to remain humble. We are to run to God and trust Him in spite of the pain. We do not have to know all of the whys but to trust God in all things.

I know what grief and suffering is all about for my precious, beautiful and holy spirit filled seventeen year old daughter Blakley, was instantly killed in a car accident December 9, 2003. She was my only child and nine months later, my mother went to be with the Lord also.

Continue to trust and praise God and He will give you peace that you and others will not be able to understand. (Philippians 4:7)

I encourage you not to mask or deny your grief. Tears are God's gift and your tears get heaven's attention! Remember, when you truly trust God, this too shall pass because of God's AMAZING GRACE. God's grace will get you through it.

The word of God calls our trials and tribulations light afflic-tion, which is but for a moment, and it worketh for us a more exceeding and external weight of glory. (2 Corinthians 4:17)

The trials and tribulation that you are going through is working for your good!

Be Blessed and Be Encouraged
You are not alone

Bettye G. Bolden
Little Rock, AR

Life is so much attitude and perception. I wrote an entire book on how we look at things and how it helps us to endure. I titled my book, "Blessings Of Cancer." It is about the story of how God in His faithfulness strengthened my family during my dad's battle with brain cancer.

God continues to use my dad's death to comfort and help others through trials and life's struggles. I'm considering changing my book title to "Finding The Rainbow After The Rain," as that is the attitude that is so desperately needed. Seeing how God can use a difficult or seemingly impossible sit-uation for His glory, and to draw people to Him, is amazing!! As we deal with life's trials and struggles it is important to always look for, and find the rainbow...after the rain. It is my prayer that you find a beautiful rainbow!

Give me a heart Lord

Give me a heart of kindness, Lord
To help those in need.
Give me a loving heart, oh Lord
Use me to plant a seed.

Give me a generous heart, my Lord
In Jesus do I trust.
I pray your love shines through me
For them, this is a must.

The trials they've gone through
I can not even begin to think,
So many life changes
Occurred in just a blink.

Life at times...seems so unfair
The pain and suffering
....it's everywhere.

But through it all
We can trust in you,
Your love and comfort
Come shining through.

Give me a heart full of grace Lord,
To understand and know it's true,
Give me a heart that's humble Lord,
And remembers to glorify you!!

Shelli Thomas
Chugiak, AK

⁓⸙⸙⸙⁓

You have suffered so much already, and many gigantic challenges still lie ahead. As you face these "giants" in the days to
come, may you be encouraged by God's Word as found in
Deuteronomy 31:6: "Be strong and courageous. Do not be
afraid or terrified because of them (the giants), for the Lord your
God goes with you, he will never leave you nor forsake you."

I know many of you have lost everything, some of you even precious loved ones, but I pray you never lose hope. When you are tempted to give up, please cling to the promise of Psalm 33:18-22: "But the eyes of the Lord are on those who fear him, on those whose hope is in his unfailing love, to deliver them from death and keep them alive in famine. We wait in hope for the Lord; he is our help and our shield. In him our hearts rejoice, for we trust in his holy name. May your unfailing love rest upon us, O Lord, even as we put our hope in you."

God's people everywhere are praying for you.

Loretta Boyett
Middleburg, FL

⁓ ⌒ ⁓

Your life is not over. What the devil meant for harm God wants to turn it into good. There is no mistake the reason your life was spared. God has a plan for your life. That's why it's important that you don't lose hope. Hope is something that we all must embrace in order to make it through this life. You may feel like that all hope is lost. You may feel as though you have nothing to live for. Let me assure you that as long as you have breath in your body you have everything to live for. You belong in this society. The society we live in today has stolen or replaced the hope that once was. Your hope is not in man or things. It's not in conditions, circumstances, feeling or emotions. Your hope is based upon Jesus Christ. We get hope from Christ in us. Hope in Jesus will push you into your destiny. Hope in the world will pull you off into sin or something that you will waste your time at. Hope is an anchor of the soul to gets you through the storms of life. What is your hope in? We don't know what tomorrow holds, but we know who holds tomorrow.

James E. Puckett
Knoxville, TN

⌒⌒⌐⌐ ⌐⌒ ⌒

God is good, He knows what He is doing and You can trust Him.

Proverbs 3:5,6 (NIV) says, "Trust in the Lord with all your heart and lean not on your own understanding; in all your ways acknowledge him and he will direct your paths." Trust in the Lord with all your heart and lean not on your own understanding. It's hard for any of us to understand a natural disaster of this magnitude and its devastation. God's ways are not our ways but He knows what is best for us. He will never let you down. He may not do things the way you expect or the way you have planned but God will take care of you. He will direct your path. He has promised us that in His Word. I want to encourage you that God is in control and He does love you very much. Lay all your concerns at His feet today and he will direct your paths in the hard days yet to come. Romans 8:28 (NIV) "And we know that all things work together for good to those who love God, to them who have been called according to his purpose."

Praying for all those affected by Hurricane Katrina!

Aimee M. Firtz
Greensburg, PA

⌒⌒⌐⌐ ⌐⌒ ⌒

My fellow New Orleanians, I share your pain and your suffering. Remember that God sends His love and comfort to us in many ways. As a girl growing up there, I could remember how our God talked to me in the trees and the sun and on the riverbanks of that wonderful city. That's where I met the Creator of the universe! He said hello to me as I rode downtown on the streetcar. He caressed my face with His mighty hand as the sun beamed down on me. Lord how You are so mighty, yet, You are so merciful! God change Your mind! Restore that wonderful city where I first met You. Show Your love to Your people! Call us to a mighty call. Allow us to heed to the divine call! Our God is shouting out to His people, LOVE ME AND LOVE MY PEOPLE! Divine Father, You are our God and we are Your people. Search us, cleanse us, and show us the way to everlasting love and life. Abba Father, Your people are desperate for You!

Jill Ijebuonwu
Snellville, GA

⌒ᘓ⸙ ⸙ᘔ⌒

"In everything give thanks, for this is the will of God in Christ Jesus for you," Thessalonians 5:18.

How beautifully this is being demonstrated by the many people rescued from hurricane "Katrina."

The expressions of joy and thanks for rescue, food, clothing and shelter, has been humbling, as seen via television, our city and church. You could never be grateful for the storm, but by your gratefulness for helping hands, we are all being touched by your loving spirit, making us more aware of all our blessings. May the Lord comfort and bless you greatly is my prayer.

Virginia Rosser
Knoxville, TN

⌒ᘓ⸙ ⸙ᘔ⌒

I took a walk one day, enjoying everything around me. The sky was blue, the air was clean, and little children were playing their normal games and families were living their normal lives. I was grateful for that moment when everything seemed to be "right". I even laughed out loud when I realized that nothing in my body was hurting and that I was so grateful to be able to walk.

That was a perfect moment.

Within days everything changed. A simple ache turned into a doctor's visit, which led to a CT scan and the news of an egg-sized tumor in my chest. For 5 weeks I endured tests, faced my greatest fears, and through it all, the Lord, my God, was right there in the middle of each second, taking away the fear that came flooding in, dealing with the "what if's" that popped into my mind, and covering me with His great sense of love at each new challenge.

I have not been in a physical flood. I have not experienced losing my house, seeing my livelihood totally disappear because of a natural disaster, however I have experienced loss of peace, loss of harmony, physical disabilities and loss of control. Yet in the middle of some of the darkest days of my life I was able to get quiet, shake off the horrible images and fears that flew into my mind, and focus on GOD!

During one of those "quiet times", the Lord spoke a very profound but quiet thought into my mind. I knew it was Him because it sure wasn't something I had ever considered... He said "Don't give power to men in high places. They are simply giving you information that I am already aware of. I AM GOD. None of this is new news to me so allow ME to walk with you through each procedure and experience.

How amazing it is to know that although God doesn't plan horrible things like tumors and natural disasters, He does allow them and yet is willing and able to walk us through them and give us a peace and sense of security that is beyond our human ability to create. Through the many procedures, biopsy, CT scans, and surgery God brought people into my life that helped me. I had to go through the process, but HE was with me and so were many wonderful doctors, nurses and friends.

The scripture that carried me through this recent challenge in my life is Isaiah 40:31 'They that wait upon the Lord will renew their strength. They will mount up with wings as eagles and they will walk and not be weary and they will run and not faint."

Four months later... I am walking again and being very grateful that God will someday allow me to RUN! The tumor was not malignant and although it was attached to my lung and I had to have a very small part of my lung removed, I am alive and very aware that the Lord got me through to where I am today.

If you have survived this terrible disaster, and you are able to read this, then there is hope. God doesn't have a magic wand that He can click and make it the way it was, however, He is able to walk you through the tough and horrible times and bring you the help that you need, day-to-day. Just let Him, and know that you are being prayed for right now!

Laurie Ecklund Long
Fresno, CA

꩜

In October of 2000 my husband and I were living in south Florida. A surprise to us and many puzzled weather forecasters, a no name storm hit our area. Torrential rain poured from the heavens with no stopping in sight. As we watched our parking lot flood and many cars (including ours) moving with the waves of the storm, we desperately tried to keep the water out from destroying our condo. A moment of fear hit me as the water entered our home faster than we could scoop it out with buckets. It was no use. We had lost the battle.

Finally mid morning the next day the water slowed down and the rain was beginning to subside. 14 inches of rain had fallen non stop and we were told that the authorities never opened the flood gates. Needless to say over 96,000 homes and businesses were destroyed in three counties. FEMA came out and declared our apartment a complete loss. It took over a year for the contractors to finish taking out the walls and install new ones, along with redoing everything from carpet to mirrors, from toilets to sinks as mildew was trying to get the best of our patience. We had no insurance other than condo insurance so many personal items were never replaced. Feeling like nomads we stood spiritually naked before the Lord. Lord why did this happen? Where are we going to go?

Feeling helpless the Lord answered our prayers. Thank God my husband's parents had mercy on us out in California. They supplied us with a roof over our head as we walked out a very long and trying year. We learned that material possessions are just that, material possessions. They can come and go as the wind. We learned how to be grateful to know that even when everything is removed from us, we still can have that personal relationship with our savior Jesus Christ. No one can take that still sweet spirit from our hearts. He is our comforter in times of need and sticks closer than a brother!

There is a song that I had put to music inspired by Psalm 93 which gave me comfort to know that God will never leave or forsake us if we put our lives in His hands.

Before the mountains were brought forth
Or ever you had formed the earth.
From everlasting, to everlasting
Thou art God.

The floods have lifted up O Lord.
The floods lift up their voice.
The Lord on high is mightier,
than the mighty waves of the sea.
Psalm 93:3-4

Debra Copeland
Dunedin, FL

⌒ᴗ₊ ₊ᴗ⌒

Tragedies such as the hurricane in New Orleans which produce much anxiety and pain is a test for humanity. Many feel
pain and hurt but all of us in our great nation feel their pain
and hurt with them. We are one family of faith and are called
upon to exhibit our faith and trust in Almighty God, whom
we serve. We willingly share our food and necessities so our
brothers may recover.

We remember the words of the Lord when He said, "I will
never leave you nor forsake you" (Heb. 13:5).

This promise gives us hope for the future.

Stanford E. Linzey, Jr.
Escondido, CA

⌒ᴗ₊ ₊ᴗ⌒

Pain is never easy to talk about, especially when there
seems to be no explanation. Sure, you know it was a Hurricane
that whipped through your community and your home, but
why? Perhaps that question will remain unanswered. If so,
don't spend your life trying to figure it out. Sometimes the
more sense we try to make out of things, the less we actually
understand about them.

One thing about God and storms is that they always seem
to show us a new side of Jesus that we've never seen before.
After The Flood of Noah's day, he garnered and treasured the
salvation of God. During the storm when Jesus was sleeping in
the boat, the disciples recognized God's sovereignty over chaos
when he uttered, "Peace be Still."

Although the Hurricane winds are gone and the flood
waters are receding, the winds and waves of emotions will continue. I can't tell you that you won't cry again. I can't promise
you that you won't weep on your front porch and shake at the

sight of what's left of your home. I can't guarantee it won't hurt. But one thing I can promise you, God will not abandon you. In fact, He's with you right now.

Your house may not be able to be rebuilt, but your home will. Streets may not be able to be fixed, but your pathway is being repaired. The Hurricane cannot wipe out your hope. The flood cannot drown your dreams. The aftermath of disaster cannot kill your will to thrive and live. With God's help, you will rise above the tide and see tomorrow's possibilities.

Though costly, perhaps this is your opportunity to see God in a whole new way; not as a God of wrath, but as a God of grace and love who spared your life. If anything, thank God that you're still here today and that he loves you unconditionally. That, my friend, is a truth that no category of Hurricane can erase.

Blessings to you,

Jacob M. Rodriguez
San Jose, CA

It's difficult to see the rainbow beyond the mulky sky
But I know it's there, cause he said it would be
Not a bird in the sky, not a sound could be heard
But I know He's there, cause he said he would be
So I ask God a question, Why?
Why have you allowed this to happen to me?
He replied, I have not forgotten you, but I choose you to be
    my special one
How special can it be to loose all you have, your house, your
    clothes your everything
He replied, my special one, I love you so much I have chosen
    you, to carry a special touch.

You will touch the lives of many you see, you've trusted me
   and now others can see
In the midst of it all, you're as strong as can be, because you
   resided in the father and the Father is in me.

Rocheroyl Lowery
Calumet City, IL

⌒⌒⊱ ⊰⌒⌒

Sometimes the Lord calms the storm, and sometimes He calms
us in the mist of the storm. God has said, "Never will I leave
you; never will I forsake you" Hebrews 13:5. He is our comfort in time of need. He has carried me through so much devastation in my life, even during times when the circumstances
made no sense to me. My prayer for you is this: may you find
comfort in the Lord and peace in His promises. Turn your face
towards God and he will turn His face towards you. Embrace
today the living word of God: "Come to Me, all who are weary
and heavy-laden, and I will give you rest. Take My yoke upon
you and learn from Me, for I am gentle and humble in heart,
and you will find rest for your souls. For My yoke is easy and
My burden is light." Matthew 11:28-30

Kimberly Alyn
San Luis Obispo, CA

⌒⌒⊱ ⊰⌒⌒

Blessed be the God and Father of our Lord Jesus Christ, the
Father of mercies and God of all comfort, who comforts us in
all our tribulation, that we may be able to comfort those who
are in any trouble, with the comfort with which we are comforted by God. 2 Corinthians 1:3-4

Last night I had a dream. Like most people, I have been watching the news coverage of the disaster in New Orleans, Mississippi, and Alabama. On one of the reports, I saw a young couple who were trying desperately to keep their family together. They had a chance to be rescued earlier, but they wanted to wait, because there was not room for the entire family in the boat that came by. So they waited, so they could all stay together. In the end, the family had to be separated. The cameras were on them, they were shown in all their misery to the entire watching world. It broke my heart to see the suffering, the agony. It impacted my very soul. To the point that - last night I had a dream.

I saw that young couple in my dream. The young wife was weeping in her despair and agony, her exhaustion evident in her face, and it was obvious she had not a shred of hope for their present circumstances, much less of hope for their future. In my dream, I saw the young husband, almost collapsing from sheer exhaustion and despair, put his arm around his wife, rock her gently back and forth and say these words to her, Don't worry, everything is going to be alright. I saw her stop crying and wipe her eyes, the tears replaced with a glimmer of hope. I saw her look around and see that there was help coming, but more than anything, I saw her leaning on her husband's reassurance and comfort.

My dream continued. Only moments later, the husband sank to the ground, collapsing onto the soggy earth beneath their feet. He put his head in his hands, and began to weep uncontrollably. The young wife, her resolve and strength renewed by the comfort he had given her, knelt beside her husband, took him in her arms, and said these words to him, Don't worry, everything is going to be alright.

There have been moments in my life when I have been in deep despair. One of those moments was when I went through a major flood. My house was waist deep in water, and when I opened the front door, I watched as some of my furniture washed down the street. It was surreal. I remembered what my mother always said, about the man crying because he had no shoes, until he saw the man who had no feet. I locked the house up and volunteered for FEMA. In doing so, I filled out paperwork for people, I listened to their stories of why they needed help. I listened to a woman tell of how her child was ripped from her arms by the water and washed away, only to be found later, drowned. I realized that I had so much to be thankful for. My house could be repaired. Things could be replaced. The woman could never get her child back, her life was changed forever in that moment. I felt inadequate. I did not know what to say. So, I put down the pencil, and walked around the table. I knelt beside the woman, then put my arms around her and said, Everything is going to be alright. I didn't know that it was, but I know that time does heal, and that God comforts us in our despair. The woman clung to me, crying, and then said, "Thank you. I needed to hear that."

How many times have I had moments where I have wanted to just have someone put their arms around me and say those words? How many times, even as a grown woman, wife, mother, and now grandmother, do I still have moments when I want to say, I want my MAMA! She was the comforter, she was the one who told me that everything was going to be alright. She was the one who first told me to depend on the Lord. That He is our Comforter. And, that life goes on, and everything will become normal again, at some point. And, you learn through every situation that you can cope. And you learn that comfort means a lot. It says that someone cares about you.

Magnify the misery and sorrow of that woman whose child was torn from her arms and swept away by the flood water. Magnify it times tens of thousands of people who have watched their loved ones die, and some who still do not know the fate of friends and family. That is what is going on in the southern gulf states right now. Tragedy, loss. Irreplaceable loss. Those people need necessities of life to sustain them on a daily basis. They need hope for a future. They need someone to comfort them in their despair. Those who have faith can rely on the word of God.

He is our Comforter. He comforts us in our time of need. We all need to show compassion. We all need to help, with prayer, with money, with our time. Everyone can help. I pray today that those of faith who are in this situation, will call upon the Lord and know that He is there. I pray that they will remember His comfort, and reach out to those around them, even if it is only to put their arms around that person, and say some simple words of comfort, Everything is going to be alright.

I pray that each of us today will get on our knees and thank God for what we have, and stop whining about the price of gasoline, and having to turn up the thermostat a bit. Everything will become normal again, at some point. Our suffering is little, compared to what these people are going through -and will continue to go through for years to come. MAY GOD BLESS YOU THIS, AND EVERY DAY

CJ Tanner
The Villages, FL

༄ ༀ ༂ ༄

You must realize and know that your God is not an impersonal, at a distance God. He is a combination of Transcendence, which means that His greatness is beyond our comprehension and Immanence, which describes His nearness to us. The One who is above everything humbled Himself and became one of us (Psalm 135:5; Philippians 2:8). In knowing this and having these truths about God deep down inside of you, it should begin to fill you with a realization that God Himself is near to you, His child, and thusly cares very deeply about you and for lack of better words, "has your back." He watches over His own in a close, loving relationship, and enables us to walk with confidence because we know that He is always with us, at all times and through all situations we face in our day.

"He will dwell on the heights, His refuge will be the impregnable rock; His bread will be given him, His water will be sure."—Isaiah 33:16

"But the LORD has been my stronghold, And my God the rock of my refuge."—Psalm 94:22

Dr. Brad Tuttle

⁀ℭ⸙ ⯊⸎⁀

So many hearts are heavy from the desolation, despair, loss... even death. Questions linger in the minds of the afflicted... How can we get through this? Why me? How can I put my life back together? Where's God when you need him most? They lay in a basement facing their darkest fears, seemingly alone. But God is not finished. There is more to the story. In an age where love is waxing cold it can be found growing, flourishing, reminding all of us that we are truly made in the image of God — in the image of Love. It is in these moments, where the strands of Man grow so strong together, that we cannot deny it. So, as the pieces are being put together we can offer an answer to at least one of these questions: "Where is God when you need him most?"
In You.
Let us all hope The Light shines bright enough to find Him in ourselves.

A L Malone
McKinney, TX

"God is Love"
...even then...

Even when...
we are surrounded by thorns,
there is a sweet breeze
caressing us,
making us whole.

Even when...
the storms are so great
they shake the trees
from their roots,
there is calm to come.

Even when...
there is war,
there are angels
whispering love.

Even when...
there is death,
there is life.

Even when ...
there is hate,
there is love.

Even where...
there is pain,
there is strength.

Even when...
there is loss,
there is gain.

Even when...
there is anger,
there is forgiveness.

Even when...
there is fear,
there is understanding.

Even where...
there is torture,
there is justice.

Even where...
there are arrows,
there is peace.

Even where...
there are tears,
there is joy.

Even when...
we are surrounded by thorns,
there are roses.

Even then...
there is
Love.

There is
Always
Love.

Always
Love.

Isabel Maria Amaya
Atlanta, GA

Printed in the United States
37831LVS00003B/145-468

9 781597 816601